IN THE DAYS OF
QUEEN ELIZABETH

IN THE DAYS OF
QUEEN ELIZABETH

BY

EVA MARCH TAPPAN

ILLUSTRATED FROM FAMOUS PAINTINGS

YESTERDAY'S CLASSICS

CHAPEL HILL, NORTH CAROLINA

This edition, first published in 2007 by Yesterday's Classics, is an unabridged republication of the work originally published by Lothrop, Lee and Shepard in 1902. For a complete listing of the books published by Yesterday's Classics, please visit www.yesterdaysclassics.com. Yesterday's Classics is the publishing arm of the Baldwin Project which presents the complete text of dozens of classic books for children at www.mainlesson.com under the editorship of Lisa M. Ripperton and T. A. Roth.

ISBN-10: 1-59915-037-9

ISBN-13: 978-1-59915-037-6

Yesterday's Classics
PO Box 3418
Chapel Hill, NC 27515

PREFACE

OF all the sovereigns that have worn the crown of England, Queen Elizabeth is the most puzzling, the most fascinating, the most blindly praised, and the most unjustly blamed. To make lists of her faults and virtues is easy. One may say with little fear of contradiction that her intellect was magnificent and her vanity almost incredibly childish; that she was at one time the most outspoken of women, at another the most untruthful; that on one occasion she would manifest a dignity that was truly sovereign, while on another the rudeness of her manners was unworthy of even the age in which she lived. Sometimes she was the strongest of the strong, sometimes the weakest of the weak.

At a distance of three hundred years it is not easy to balance these claims to censure and to admiration, but at least no one should forget that the little white hand of which she was so vain guided the ship of state with most consummate skill in its perilous passage through the troubled waters of the latter half of the sixteenth century.

EVA MARCH TAPPAN

Worcester, March, 1902

CONTENTS

CHAPTER I

THE BABY PRINCESS

TWO ladies of the train of the Princess Elizabeth were talking softly together in an upper room of Hunsdon House.

"Never has such a thing happened in England before," said the first.

"True," whispered the second, "and to think of a swordsman being sent for across the water to Calais! That never happened before."

"Surely no good can come to the land when the head of her who has worn the English crown rolls in the dust at the stroke of a French executioner," murmured the first lady, looking half fearfully over her shoulder.

"But if a queen is false to the king, if she plots against the peace of the throne, even against the king's very life, why should she not meet the same punishment that the wife of a tradesman would suffer if she strove to bring death to her husband? The court declared that Queen Anne was guilty."

"Yes, the court, the court," retorted the first, "and what a court! If King Henry should say, 'Cranmer, cut off your father's head,' and 'Cromwell, cut off your mother's head,' they would bow humbly before him and answer, 'Yes, sire,' provided only that they could have wealth in one hand and power in the other. A court, yes!"

"Oh, well, I'm to be in the train of the Princess Elizabeth, and I'm not the one to sit on the judges' bench and say whether the death that her mother died yesterday was just or unjust," said the second lady with a little yawn. "But bend your head a bit nearer," she went on, "and I'll tell you what the lord mayor of London whispered to a kinsman of my own. He said there was neither word nor sign of proof against her that was the queen, and that he who had but one eye could have seen that King Henry wished to get rid of her. But isn't that your brother coming up the way?"

"Yes, it is Ralph. He is much in the king's favor of late because he can play the lute so well and can troll a poem better than any other man about the court. He will tell us of the day in London."

Ralph had already dismounted when his sister came to the hall, too eager to welcome him to wait for any formal announcement of his arrival.

"Greeting, sister Clarice," said he as he kissed her cheek lightly. "How peaceful it all is on this quiet hill with trees and flowers about, and breezes that bring the echoes of bird-notes rather than the noise and tumult of the city."

"But I am sure that I heard one sound of the city yesterday, Ralph. It was the firing of a cannon just at twelve. Was not that the hour when the stroke of the French ruffian beheaded the queen? Were there no murderers in England that one must needs be sent for across the water?"

"I had hardly thought you could hear the sound so far," said her brother, "but it was as you say. The cannon was the signal that the deed was done."

"And where was King Henry? Was he within the Tower? Did he look on to make sure that the swordsman had done his work?"

"Not he. No fear has King Henry that his servants will not obey him. He was in Epping Forest on a hunt. I never saw him more full of jest, and the higher the sun rose, the merrier he became. We went out early in the morning, and the king bade us stop under an oak tree to picnic. The wine was poured out, and we stood with our cups raised to drink his health. It was an uproarious time, for while the foes of the Boleyns rejoiced, their friends dared not be otherwise than wildly merry, lest the wrath of the king be visited upon them. He has the eye of an eagle to pierce the heart of him who thinks the royal way is not the way of right."

"The wine would have choked me," said Clarice, "but go on, Ralph. What next?"

"One of the party slipped on the root of the oak, and his glass fell on a rock at his feet. The jesting stopped for an instant, and just at that moment came the boom of a cannon from the Tower. King Henry had forbidden the hour of the execution to be told, but every one guessed that the cannon was the signal that the head of Queen Anne had been struck off by the foreign swordsman. The king turned white and then red. I was nearest him, and I saw him tremble. I followed his eye, and he looked over the shoulder of the master of the hunt far away to the eastward. There was London, and up the spire of St. Paul's a flag was slowly rising. It looked very small from that distance, but it was another signal that the stroke of the executioner had been a true one."

"It is an awful thing to take the life of one who has worn the crown," murmured Clarice. "Did the king speak?"

"He half opened his lips and again closed them. Then he gave a laugh that made me shiver, and he said, 'One would think that the royal pantry could afford no extra glass. That business is finished. Unloose the dogs, and let us follow the boar.' Greeting, Lady Margaret," said Ralph to a lady who just then entered the room. He bowed before her with deep respect, and said in a low, earnest tone:—

"May you find comfort and courage in every trouble that comes to you."

Lady Margaret's eyes filled with tears as she said:—

"I thank you. Trouble has, indeed, come to me in these last few years. Where was the king yesterday— at the hour of noon, I mean? Had he the heart to stay in London?"

4

"He had the heart to go on a hunt, but it was a short one, and almost as soon as the cannon was fired, he set off on the hardest gallop that ever took man over the road from Epping Forest to Wiltshire."

"To the home of Sir John Seymour?"

"The same. Know you not that this morning before the bells rang for noon Jane Seymour had taken the place of Anne Boleyn and become the wife of King Henry?"

"No, I knew it not," answered Lady Margaret, "but what matters a day sooner or later when a man goes from the murder of one wife to the wedding of another?"

"True," said Ralph. Clarice was sobbing softly, and Lady Margaret went on, half to Ralph and half to herself:—

"It was just two years ago yesterday when Lady Anne set out for London to be crowned. I never saw the Thames so brilliant. Every boat was decked with flags and streamers, edged with tiny bells that swung and tinkled in the breeze. The boats were so close together that it was hard to clear a way for the lord mayor's barge. All the greatest men of London were with him. They wore scarlet gowns and heavy golden chains. On one side of the lord mayor was a boat full of young men who had sworn to defend Queen Anne to the death. Just ahead was a barge loaded with cannon, and their mouths pointed in every direction that the wind blows. There was a great dragon, too, so cunningly devised that it would twist and turn one way and then another, and wherever it turned, it spit red fire and green and blue into the river. There was another boat full of the fairest maidens in London town, and they all sang songs in praise of the Queen."

"They say that Queen Anne, too, could make songs," said Ralph, "and that she made one in prison that begins:—

> 'Oh, Death, rock me asleep.
> Bring on my quiet rest.' "

"When Anne Boleyn went to France with the sister of King Henry, she was a merry, innocent child. At his door lies the sin of whatever of wrong she has done," said Lady Margaret solemnly, half turning away from Clarice and her brother and looking absently out of the open window. The lawn lay before her, fresh and green. Here and there were daisies, gleaming in the May sunshine. "I know the very place," said she with a shudder. "It is the green within the Tower. The grass is fresh and bright there, too, but the daisies will be red to-day with the blood of our own crowned queen. It is terrible to think of the daisies."

"Pretty daisies," said a clear, childish voice under the window.

"Let us go out on the lawn," said Clarice, "it stifles me here."

"Remember," bade Lady Margaret hastily, "to say 'Lady,' not 'Princess.' "

The young man fell upon one knee before a tiny maiden, not yet three years old. The child gravely extended her hand for him to kiss. He kissed it and said:—

"Good morrow, my Lady Elizabeth."

"Princess 'Lizbeth," corrected the mite.

"No," said Lady Margaret, "not 'Princess' but 'Lady.'"

"Princess 'Lizbeth," insisted the child with a stamp of her baby foot on the soft turf and a positive little shake of her red gold curls. "Princess brought you some daisies," and with a winning smile she held out the handful of flowers to Lady Margaret and put up her face to be kissed.

"I'll give you one," said the child to the young man, and again she extended her hand to him.

"Princess 'Lizbeth wants to go to hear the birds sing. Take me," she bade the attendant. She made the quaintest little courtesy that can be imagined, and left the three standing under the great beech tree.

"That is our Lady Elizabeth," said Lady Margaret, "the most wilful, winsome little lassie in all the world."

"But why may she not be called 'Princess' as has been the custom?" asked Ralph.

"It is but three days, indeed, since the king's order was given," answered Lady Margaret. "When Archbishop Cranmer decided that Anne Boleyn was not the lawful wife of Henry, the king declared that Princess Elizabeth should no longer be the heir to the throne, and so should be called 'Lady' instead of 'Princess.' It is many months since he has done aught for her save to provide for her safe keeping here at Hunsdon. The child lacks many things that every child of quality should have, let alone that she be the daughter of a king. I dare not tell the king her needs, lest he be angry, and both the little one and myself feel his wrath."

The little daughter of the king seems to have been entirely neglected, and at last Lady Margaret ventured to write, not to the king, but to Chancellor Cromwell, to lay before him her difficulties. Here is part of her letter:—

"Now it is so, my Lady Elizabeth is put from that degree she was afore, and what degree she is at now, I know not but by hearsay. Therefore I know not how to order her myself, nor none of hers that I have the rule of, that is, her women and grooms, beseeching you to be good Lord to my good Lady and to all hers, and that she may have some raiment." The letter goes on to say that she has neither gown, nor slip, nor petticoat, nor kerchiefs, nor neckerchiefs, nor nightcaps, "nor no manner of linen," and ends, "All these her Grace must have. I have driven off as long as I can, that by my troth I can drive it off no longer. Beseeching ye, mine own good Lord, that ye will see that her Grace may have that which is needful for her, as my trust is that ye will do."

The little princess had a good friend in Lady Margaret Bryan, the "lady mistress" whom Queen Anne had put over her when, as the custom was, the royal baby was taken from her mother to dwell in another house with her own retinue of attendants and ladies in waiting. In this same letter the kind lady mistress ventured to praise the neglected child. She wrote of her:—

"She is as toward a child and as gentle of condition as ever I knew any in my life. I trust the king's Grace shall have great comfort in her Grace." Lady Margaret told the chancellor that the little one was having "great pain with her great teeth." Probably the last thing that King Henry thought of was showing his daughter to the public or making her prominent in any way, but the lady mistress sturdily suggested that if he should wish it, the Lady Elizabeth would be so taught that she would be an honor to the king, but she must not be kept too long before the public, she must have her freedom again in a day or two.

A small difficulty arose in the house itself. The steward of the castle wished the child to dine at the state table instead of at her own more simple board.

"It is only fitting," said he, "for her to dine at the great table, since she is at the head of the house."

"Master Steward," declared Lady Margaret, "at the state table there would be various meats and fruits and wines that would not be for her good. It would be a hard matter for me to keep them from her when she saw them at every meal."

"Teach her that she may not have all that she sees," said the steward.

"The table of state is no place for the correcting of children," retorted Lady Margaret, and she wrote to

9

the chancellor about this matter also. "I know well," said she, "if she [Elizabeth] be at the table of state, I shall never bring her up to the king's Grace's honor nor hers, nor to her health. Wherefore I beseech you, my Lord, that my Lady may have a mess of meat to her own lodging, with a good dish or two that is meet for her Grace to eat of."

Besides the Lady Elizabeth and her household, the lady mistress, the steward, the ladies of her train, and the servants, there was one other dweller in this royal nursery, and that was the Lady Mary, a half-sister of the little Elizabeth. Mary's mother had been treated very cruelly and unfairly by King Henry, and had finally been put away from him that he might marry Anne Boleyn.

As a child Mary was shown more honor than had ever been given to an English princess before. The palace provided for her residence was carried on at an enormous expense. She had her own ladies in waiting, her chamberlain, treasurer, and chaplain, as if she were already queen. Even greater than this was her glory when on one occasion her father and mother were absent in France, for she was taken to her father's palace, and there the royal baby of but three or four years represented all the majesty of the throne. The king's councilors reported to him that when some gentlemen of note went to pay their respects at the English court, they found this little child in the presence chamber with her guards and attendants, and many noble ladies most handsomely apparelled. The councilors said that she welcomed her guests and entertained them with all propriety, and that finally she condescended to play for them on the virginals, an instrument with keys like those of a piano. If half this story is true, it is no wonder that the delighted courtiers told the king they "greatly marvelled and rejoiced."

The following Christmas she spent with her father and mother. She had most valuable presents of all sorts of articles made of gold and silver; cups, saltcellars, flagons, and—strangest of all gifts for a little child—a pair of silver snuffers. One part of the Christmas celebration must have pleased her, and that was the acting of several plays by a company of children who had been carefully trained to entertain the little princess.

When Mary was but six years old, it was arranged that she should marry the German emperor, Charles V. He came to England for the betrothal, and remained several weeks. Charles ruled over more territory than any other sovereign of the times, and he was a young man of great talent and ability. The child must be educated to become an empress. Being a princess was no longer all play. A learned Spaniard wrote a profound treatise on the proper method of training the little girl. He would allow her to read the writings of some of the Latin poets and orators and philosophers, and she might read history, but no romances. A Latin grammar was written expressly for her, and she must also study French and music. There seems to have been little thought of her recreation save that it was decreed that she might "use moderate exercise at seasons convenient."

So it was that the pretty, merry little maiden was trained to become an empress. When she was ten years old, she sent Charles an emerald ring, asking him whether his love was still true to her. He returned a tender message that he would wear the ring for her sake; and yet, the little girl to whom he had been betrothed never became the bride of the emperor.

Charles heard that King Henry meant to put away his wife, and if that was done, it was probable that Mary would no longer be "Princess of Wales," and would never inherit her father's kingdom. The emperor was angry, and the little girl in the great, luxurious palace was hurt and grieved.

This was the beginning of the hard life that lay before her. King Henry was determined to be free from his wife that he might make Anne Boleyn his queen. Mary loved her mother with all her heart, but the king refused to allow them to see each other. The mother wrote most tenderly to her child, bidding her be cheerful and obey the king in everything that was not wrong. Mary's seventeenth birthday came and went. The king had accomplished his wish to put away his wife, and had made Anne Boleyn his queen. One September day their child Elizabeth was born. So far Mary had lived in the greatest state, surrounded by attendants who delighted in showing deference to her wishes, and her only unhappiness had been caused by the separation from her mother and sympathy with her mother's sufferings. One morning the chamberlain, John Hussey, came to her with downcast eyes.

"Your Grace," said he, "it is but an hour ago that a message came from his Majesty, the king, and——" His voice trembled, and he could say no more.

"Speak on, my good friend," said Mary. "I can, indeed, hardly expect words of cheer from the court that is ruled by her who was once my mother's maid of honor, but tell me to what purport is the message?"

"No choice have I but to speak boldly and far more harshly than is my wish," replied the chamberlain, "and I crave your pardon for saying what I would so gladly leave unsaid. I would that the king had named some other agent."

"But what is the message, my good chamberlain? Must I command it to be told to me? My mother's daughter knows no fear. I am strong to meet whatever is to come."

"The king commands through his council," said the chamberlain in a choking voice, "that your Grace shall no longer bear the title of 'Princess,' for that belongs henceforth to the child of himself and Queen Anne. He bids that you shall order your servants to address you as 'Lady Mary,' and that you shall remove at once to Hunsdon, the palace of the Princess Elizabeth, for she it is who is to be his heir and is to inherit the kingdom."

"I thank you," said Mary calmly, "for the courtesy with which you have delivered the message; but I am the daughter of the king, and without his own letter I refuse to believe that he would be minded to diminish the state and rank of his eldest child."

A few days later there came a letter from an officer of the king's household bidding her remove to the palace of the child Elizabeth.

"I will not accept the letter as the word of my father," declared Mary. "It names me as 'Lady Mary' and not as 'Princess';" and she straightway wrote, not to the council, but directly to the king:—

"I will obey you as I ought, and go whereever you bid me, but I cannot believe that your Grace knew of this letter, since therein I am addressed as 'Lady Mary.' To accept this title would be to declare that I am not your eldest child, and this my conscience will not permit." She signs herself, "Your most humble daughter, Mary, Princess."

King Henry was angry, and when Queen Anne came to him in tears and told him a fortune-teller had predicted that Mary should rule after her father, he declared that he would execute her rather than allow such a thing to happen. Parliament did just what he commanded, and now he bade that an act be passed settling the crown upon the child of Queen Anne. Mary's luxurious household of more than eightscore attendants was broken up, and she herself was sent to Hunsdon. Many of her attendants accompanied her, but they were bidden to look no longer upon her as their supreme mistress. They were to treat the child Elizabeth as Princess of Wales and heir to the throne of England.

CHAPTER II

THE CHILD ELIZABETH

I T was a strange household at Hunsdon, a baby ruler with crowds of attendants to do her honor and obey her slightest whim. Over all was the strong hand of the king, and his imperious will to which every member of the house yielded save the one slender girl who paid no heed to his threats, but stood firmly for her mother's rights and her own.

For more than two years all honor was shown to the baby Elizabeth, but on the king's marriage to Jane Seymour, he commanded his obedient Parliament to decree that Elizabeth should never wear the crown, and that, if Jane had no children, the king might will his kingdom to whom he would. To the little child the change in her position was as yet a small matter, but to the young girl of twenty-one years the future seemed very dark. Her mother had died, praying in vain that the king would grant her but one hour with her beloved daughter. Mary was fond of study and spent much of the time with her books. Visitors were rare, for few ventured to brave the wrath of Henry VIII., but one morning it was announced that Lady Kingston awaited her Grace.

"I give you cordial greeting," said Mary. "You were ever true to me, and in these days it is but seldom that I meet a faithful friend."

"A message comes to your Grace through me that will, I hope, give you some little comfort," said Lady Kingston.

"From my father?" cried Mary eagerly.

"No, but from one whose jealous dislike may have done much to turn the king against you, from her who was Anne Boleyn. The day before her death," continued Lady Kingston, "she whispered to me, 'I have something to say to you alone.' She sent away her attendants and bade me follow her into the presence chamber of the Tower. She locked and bolted the door with her own hand. Then she commanded, 'Sit you down in the royal seat.' I said, 'Your Majesty, in your presence it is my duty to stand, not to sit, much less to sit in the seat of the queen.' She shook her head and said sadly, 'I am no longer the queen. I am but a poor woman condemned to die to-morrow. I pray you be seated.' It seemed a strange wish, but she was so earnest that I obeyed. She fell upon her knees at my feet and said, 'Go you to Mary, my stepdaughter, fall down before her feet as I now fall before yours, and beg her humbly to pardon the wrong that I have done her. This is my message.' "

Mary was silent. Then she said slowly:—

"Save for her, my mother's life and my own would have been full of happiness, but I forgive her as I hope to be forgiven. The child whom she has left to suffer, it may be, much that I have suffered, shall be to me as a sister—and truly, she is a winsome little maiden." Mary's face softened at the thought of the baby Elizabeth.

She kept her word, and it was but a few weeks before Mary, who had once been bidden to look up to the child as her superior, was generously trying to arouse her father's interest in his forsaken little daughter. Henry VIII., cruel as he showed himself, was always eager to have people think well of him, and in his selfish, tyrannical fashion, he was really fond of his children. Mary had been treated most harshly, but she longed to meet him. Her mother was dead, she was alone. If he would permit her to come to him, it might be that he would show her the same kindness and affection as when she was a child. She wrote him submissive letters, and finally he consented to pardon her for daring to oppose his will. Hardly was she assured of his forgiveness before she wrote:—

"My sister Elizabeth is in good health, thanks to our Lord, and such a child as I doubt not but your Highness shall have cause to rejoice of in time coming."

The months went by, and when Elizabeth was about four years old, a message came from the king to say that a son was born to him, and that the two princesses were bidden to come to the palace to attend the christening.

Such a celebration it was! The queen was wrapped in a mantle of crimson velvet edged with ermine. She was laid upon a kind of sofa on which were many cushions of damask with border of gold. Over her was spread a robe of fine scarlet cloth with a lining of ermine. In the procession, the baby son was carried in the arms of a lady of high rank under a canopy borne by four nobles. Then came other nobles, one bearing a great wax candle, some with towels about their necks, and some bringing bowls and cups, all of solid gold, as gifts for the child who was to inherit the throne of England. A long line of servants and attendants followed. The Princess Mary wore a robe of cloth of silver trimmed with pearls. Every motion of hers was watched, for she was to be godmother to the little child. There was another young maiden who won even more attention than the baby prince, and this was the four-year-old Princess Elizabeth. She was dressed in a robe of state with as long a train as any of the ladies of the court. In her hand she carried a golden vase containing the chrism, or anointing oil, and she herself was borne in the arms of the queen's brother. She had been sound asleep when the time came to make ready for the ceremony, for the christening took place late in the evening, and the procession set out with the light of many torches flashing upon the jewels of the nobles and ladies of rank and upon the golden cups and bowls.

Along the wide hall and down the grand staircase went the glittering line. The baby was christened "Edward," and then was proclaimed "the beloved son of our most dread and gracious Lord, Henry VIII." On the return the little Elizabeth walked beside Mary, keeping fast hold of her sister's hand, while the long train was borne by a noble lady of the court. The trumpet sounded all the way back to the royal bed-chamber where lay the queen, waiting to greet her son with her blessing. It was midnight, and Elizabeth as well as her baby brother must have been glad to be allowed to rest.

Only a few days later came the death of the mother of the little prince. Greatly as King Henry disliked black, he wore it for four months, even on Christmas day. Elizabeth was probably at Hunsdon, but Mary spent Christmas with her father. She did not forget the little sister, but sent her a box decorated with silver needlework made by her own hand. She gave the baby brother a cap which must have been very elaborate, for it cost enough to pay the wages of a working man for four months. To the baby's nurse she sent a bonnet that cost half as much as the cap. Another gift, which she herself made, was a cushion covered with rich embroidery.

This baby brother was a delight to both the princesses. Mary went often to see him, and looked after him as if he had been her own child, and to Elizabeth he was the most precious thing in all the world. "I pray you, take me to see my brother," she often pleaded. One day the older sister said to her, "Elizabeth, is there aught that I can do to please you greatly?"

"I would gladly go to see my brother," was the child's answer.

"That cannot well be," said Mary. "Is there nothing better that you can wish?"

"No, sister."

"But there is surely one thing better. When it is two of the clock, stand you close by the west window of the hall, and what is to come will come."

Clocks were not very common in those days, but there was one in the hall at Hunsdon, and the excited little girl watched the hands move slowly around until they marked the hour of two. What was to come?

A little after two a single rider appeared. "Make way for his Grace, Edward, Prince of Wales!" he cried. Then came the trumpeters and, following them, the nobles. After the nobles came the royal baby for whom all this ceremonial had been arranged. He lay in the arms of his nurse, "Mother Jack," and was borne in a litter. The upright poles were heavily gilded, and the canopy was of the richest white silk edged with a golden fringe. Clusters of white plumes were fixed at each corner. On the shoulders of eight men rested the shafts of the chair. All around it gathered noble lords and ladies, mounted on horses whose trappings were marked with the monogram of many a family of rank and power. Every man wore a sword to defend the heir of England's king, if need should arise, and stalwart guards marched on either side.

"It's my own little brother," cried Elizabeth.

"And he comes to abide with us for a while," said Mary. "Is not that better, my little sister, than going to him to pay a visit of a day?"

"Will Lady Margaret grant me leave to show him my birds and my rabbits? He shall play on my virginals, if he will; and, truly, I'll not mind the sharp prick of the needle, if I may but sew a dress for him. I would fain learn to make letters with the needle, sister Mary, that I might sew one all myself on everything that he will wear. Oh, it will be an 'E,' even as it is on whatever is mine."

It is quite possible that the next few years were the happiest that Elizabeth ever knew. She was four years older than Edward, and she had been so carefully trained by Lady Margaret that King Henry was glad that she should be the playmate of the sweet-tempered little fellow who was his only son and heir. Lady Margaret was troubled because Edward's best coat was "only tinsel" instead of cloth of gold, and because he had "never a good jewel to set on his cap;" but this was nothing to the little prince so long as he had his sister. Lady Margaret wrote to the king that she wished he could have seen the prince, for "the minstrels played, and his Grace danced and played so wantonly that he could not stand still." Elizabeth taught him to speak, and for his sake she even conquered her dislike to the "prick of the needle," for when his second birthday came and the rich nobles of the kingdom sent him jewels and all sorts of beautiful things made of gold and silver, she gave him a tiny cambric shirt, every stitch of which had been made by the little fingers of his six-year-old sister. Mary sent him a cloak of crimson satin. The sleeves were of tinsel. It was heavily embroidered with gold thread and with pansies made of pearls.

It was about this time that King Henry sent an officer of high rank expressly to bestow the royal blessing upon the two princesses. On his return he reported to the king the grateful message that Mary had sent.

"And how found you her Grace, the Lady Elizabeth?" asked King Henry.

"Truly, your Majesty," replied the chancellor, "were the Lady Elizabeth not the offspring of your illustrious Highness, I could in no way account for her charm of manner and of speech. 'I humbly thank his most excellent Majesty,' she said, 'that he has graciously deigned to think upon me, who am verily his loving child and his true and faithful subject.' "

"She is but six years old," mused Henry. "Were those her words?"

"I would gladly have had pen and paper," answered the chancellor, "that no one of them should have been lost, but I give the message as it has remained in my memory. She asked after your Majesty's welfare with as great a gravity as she had been forty years old."

More than one trouble came to the older princess. Soon after the king had sent his blessing to the two sisters, a councilor came to Mary with a message of quite another character.

"It is his Majesty's pleasure," said he, "that your Grace should receive the Duke Philip of Germany as a suitor for your hand." This German duke was a Protestant, and Mary was a firm Roman Catholic, but she dared not refuse to obey the king's bidding.

"I would gladly remain single," said she, "but I am bound to obey his Majesty. I would, too, that the duke were of my own faith, but in so weighty a matter I can do naught save to commit myself to my merciful father and most sovereign lord, knowing that his goodness and wisdom will provide for me far better than I could make protection for myself."

The duke sent her a beautiful diamond cross, but before a year had passed, she was bidden by the King to return the gift. Henry had wedded a German wife, and had treated her so badly that Mary's betrothal was broken.

There were sad times in England in those days. When Henry VIII. wished to marry Anne Boleyn, he asked the Pope to declare that his marriage to the mother of Mary was not lawful. The Pope refused. Henry then asked the opinion of several universities in England, Italy, and France, and it is probable that his question was accompanied by either bribes or threats. The universities declared the first marriage unlawful; but the Pope would not yield. Henry then declared that the English church should be free from the Pope, and that the king himself was properly the supreme head of the church in his own kingdom.

There were tyrants, and most cruel tyrants before the days of Henry VIII., but they were generally satisfied to rule men's deeds. Henry was determined to rule his subjects' most secret thoughts. If he suspected that a man did not believe that his divorce was right, he would pursue the man and force him to express his opinion. If the man was too honest to tell a falsehood, he was imprisoned or executed, for Henry said that it was treason to refuse to acknowledge that the king of

England was at the head of the church of England. Many of the noblest, truest men in the land were put to death for this reason. This was not all, for although Henry would not acknowledge the authority of the Pope, he nevertheless declared that he was a Roman Catholic, and that all Protestants were heretics and deserved to be burned to death. The result of this strange reasoning was that if a man was a Protestant, he ran the risk of being burned at the stake, while if he was a Roman Catholic, he was in danger of being hanged.

Mary was often at the court. She must have heard her father's brutal threats against all those who did not love his will. One after another of her childhood's friends was beheaded or burned at the stake; her old teacher, her mother's chaplain, and the beloved countess to whose care her mother had confided her as an infant. Not a word or look of criticism might she venture, for the despot would hardly have hesitated to send his own daughter to the stake if she had dared to resist him in this matter.

The case was quite different with Elizabeth and Edward. They knew little of burnings and executions. Whatever of gentleness and kindness was in King Henry was shown to the children, especially to his son. The little ones played and studied together. "My sweetest and dearest sister" was the little boy's name for Elizabeth. She was a favorite wherever she went. The king married three times after the death of Jane Seymour, and each of these stepmothers was fond of the merry, pleasing little girl.

The first of the three was the German princess. She was rather slow and dull, and Henry took a great dislike to her. When the little Elizabeth, then about seven years old, begged to be allowed to come to court to see the queen, King Henry roared, "Tell her that her own mother was so different from this woman that she ought not to wish to see her." This was the only time that he ever spoke of Anne Boleyn.

Elizabeth met the new stepmother after a short delay, and this lady was so charmed with the little maiden that she begged to see much of her, the only favor that she ever asked of the king. The next wife was a distant relative of Anne Boleyn, and when she dined in public, she gave the place opposite herself to the child. "She is of my own blood," said the queen, "and it is only right that she should be next to me."

At Henry's last marriage Mary and the two children were present, and this new queen became like the others a warm friend of Elizabeth, who was now fully ten years old. Henry must have felt some affection for Anne Boleyn, for he was never displeased to hear the praises of her daughter. He seemed beginning to have a real fondness for the child, and one day he looked at her keenly and said:—

"There's more than one that would be glad to have you. Would you be married, Elizabeth, or would you stay with your books and birds and viols and lutes?"

"I would fain do that which your Majesty bids," answered the child. "I know well that what your Majesty commands is ever the thing which is best."

"She's a child of wisdom," declared Henry with a smile of gratification, "and I'll do more for her than anyone can guess." Then said he to Elizabeth:—

"It shall be brought about that you shall become the bride of some great man. If any German Emperor plays you false, he shall feel the weight of my hand. How would it please your Grace to marry a prince of Portugal?" he asked playfully, for he was in a rarely good humor, "Or perhaps, Philip of Spain? Philip will be a king, and he would make you a great lady. Would it please you to wed one that would make you a queen?"

"Far rather would I wed one that I could make a king," answered the child, drawing herself up to her full height.

"What!" cried the king, his face changing in a moment, and his eyes flashing ominously. The girl seemed looking not at the king, but far away into some distant future. She did not see the warning glance of the queen.

"I would fain be so beautiful and so great," said she, "that whoever came near me should admire me and should beg me to become his wife. I would say no to one and all, but by and by I would choose one for myself. Him I would raise to be as great as I, and I would——" Elizabeth of England, even as a child, rarely forgot herself, but she was absorbed in the picture that she was making, and she stopped only when she felt the silence and saw her father's wrathful gaze fixed upon her. His eyes were fairly blazing with anger, and his face was purple.

"So that is what you plan, is it?" he roared. "And here you stand before me and tell your schemes to become queen and raise some miserable rascal to the throne. Get out of my sight, ingrate that you are."

Quick-witted as Elizabeth was, she did not at once see wherein she was in fault. She was so dazed by this sudden fury that she did not even think to throw herself at the feet of the king and beg to be forgiven, even though she knew not for what. The stepmother pleaded, "Pardon the child, my king. She meant no wrong."

"No wrong," thundered the king. "Is it 'no wrong' to plan what she will do as soon as the breath is out of her father's body? I tell you, girl that you may find another father and another throne, for never shall you sit upon mine. Get to your litter, and do you never come before my eyes again."

The little Edward had slipped up softly behind his angry father and had laid his tiny hand upon the king's purple cheek.

"Your Majesty is naughty," he declared bravely, "You have made my sweetest sister cry. I don't want my sister to cry." Never had the little boy received a harsh word from his father, and he was perhaps the only one in the kingdom who had no fear of the king. "Come," said he, "and tell her not to cry." He caught the king by the hand, but even for his son King Henry's anger could not be suppressed.

"You little know her," he said. "It is you that she would rob. She would seize upon the place that is your own and drive you from it. Tell her to depart from the palace and never enter it," he commanded his chamberlain, and soon the little girl, not yet twelve years old, was sent away from the court in disgrace.

"Hold yourself with patience," whispered the queen to the child. "Trust me, and believe that it shall not be long before you will again be sent for."

CHAPTER III

A BOY KING

T HE queen did all in her power for the little offender, but it was a whole year before she was again allowed to come to court. There was war in France, and the king sailed away in his ship with its sails of cloth of gold, apparently forgetting all about the little daughter whom he had left without a word of farewell. The child dared not write him, but she wrote the queen a grateful little Italian letter. "I feel bound not only to be obedient to you," she said, "but also to look up to you with filial love, and chiefly because I learn that you, most illustrious Highness, never forget me in your letters to his Majesty, the king." Then she begged the queen when writing the king, always to speak of her. "Commend me to him with my continual prayer that he will give me his kind blessing," pleaded the anxious child.

After keeping his anger for a whole year, the king finally deigned to send his blessing to "all" his children. The poor little girl was comforted, and made so happy by this tardy forgiveness that she cast gratefully about her to see what she could do to show her gratitude to the kind stepmother who had done so much to appease his wrath. She knew of a little French book that was a favorite of the queen's, and this she translated into English and sent to her. The cover was embroidered in blue and silver, and there was a quaint little dedication saying that she knew nothing in it "was done as it should have been." It is no wonder that the grateful child became a great favorite with her kind-hearted stepmother.

Henry was successful in France; England had been well governed by the queen during his absence; he was on good terms with all his family; and although there had been a visitation of the plague, his children were safe. It was probably at this happy time that a large picture was painted of Henry, his three children, and the mother of Edward. The king sits on a kind of dais with Jane Seymour beside him. He is gorgeous in scarlet and gold brocade, and his two daughters equally dazzling in their crimson velvet and cloth of gold. The precious little prince stands at his father's right hand, and the king's arm is thrown around the child's neck. Both king and prince wear velvet caps; each with a long white plume. Gold chains and rubies and pearls are everywhere.

Queen Katherine does not appear in the picture, but she had a strong hold on the daily lives of the royal family. She saw to it that so far as lay in her power the neglected elder daughter should have the position that belonged to her. Princess as she was, Mary never had after her mother's divorce an allowance half large enough to do what was expected of her, but now she was helped in many ways by the thoughtful step-mother. The queen would send a handsome gown or a generous gift of money, or she would arrange to pension off some some aged, helpless servant of Mary's, and so lessen the demands upon the girl's slender purse. She was little older than the princess, but she showed a motherly watchfulness of Mary's interests.

No less thoughtful was she of the training of her younger stepchildren. It was the fashion for young people of rank to be highly educated, especially in the languages, and if half the reports of the knowledge acquired by the two children are true, they must have been wonderfully industrious students. One who knew them well declared that they called for their books as soon as it was light. First came the reading of the Scriptures, then breakfast, and after that the study of various languages. When the long hours of work were over, the little prince was allowed to exercise in the open air, while Elizabeth "betook herself to her lute or viol, and when wearied with these, employed her time in needle-work." Four or five modern languages this industrious princess learned to speak and write. She had some knowledge of Greek, and she spoke Latin almost as easily as English. A little book in which she wrote her Italian exercises is still in existence. They are well written, but there are mistakes enough to show that even a princess does not learn a language without hard work.

Both children had a great admiration for Queen Katherine, and whatever she did was right in their eyes. Edward seems to have had as hard a time learning to write as any child of to-day, and he sent a letter to the queen about his troubles. "When I see your beautiful handwriting," says the discouraged little boy, "I am sick of writing. But then I think how kind your nature is, and that whatever proceeds from a good mind and intention will be acceptable, and so I write you this letter."

The gentle boy, not yet nine years old, was soon to be put forward to represent the king. Henry had grown so enormously stout that he could not climb the stairs. After a while he could no longer even walk about his room, and he had to be moved in a rolling chair. Commissioners from the king of France were coming to England to arrange terms of peace. The king ordered his son to take his place.

"Your Majesty," reported the officer in whose charge the child had been, "truly, never was there a prince of such courtesy and amiability. His Grace rode on the charger most gallantly, and led the two thousand knights and nobles with as much of ease and stateliness of demeanor as if he had been forty years of age."

"And did he speak as he was taught?" asked the king.

"Surely, your Majesty, and with such grace and sovereignty in his manner that men were affected even to tears."

"And what said the admiral?"

"I verily believe, your Highness, that he would have caught up the prince's Grace and clasped him to his breast had it not been for the dignity of his Grace's manner and bearing. He put his arm about the neck of his Grace, but it was a kiss of affection and not of state that he gave."

"And after that?"

"After the speech of welcome, my lord prince again took the head of the cavalcade. Never before the time of your Majesty have they been handled by such a leader. He led the French away from the Heath to meet your Highness's gracious welcome at the palace."

The boy was not spoiled by all this honor and praise, but went willingly away from the glories of the court to stay with his beloved sister Elizabeth. Less than a year were they together, and then it was thought best for them to be separated. Edward was but a lonely little child in spite of his stateliness when on the great charger, and he grieved so for his sister that she wrote to him suggesting that they write frequent letters to each other. The boy caught eagerly at the idea. "Nothing can now occur to me more grateful than your letters," he wrote in the prim, stilted fashion of the day, and he added, "It is a comfort to my regret that I hope shortly to see you again if no accident intervenes." He did see her again before many weeks had passed, for there was news to tell which the councilors wished both children to hear.

King Henry had been growing more and more feeble. For some time before his death, it was so difficult for him to sign his name that three men, acting together, were given the right to do it for him. Two made an impression of his signature with a dry stamp, and the third traced the letters with ink. Henry grew no less bitter in his enmity to all who opposed him, and one of his last acts was to order the execution of his aunt's husband.

One winter day two men galloped swiftly over the road to the palace which was then the home of Edward.

"Inform his Highness that the Duke of Somerset and Sir Anthony Brown await his pleasure," was the message brought to the prince. The Duke of Somerset was Edward's mother's brother, and he went eagerly to meet his guests.

"I rejoice that you bring me word of his Majesty," said the boy. "Is it not yet his will that I should come to him?"

"Your Grace," answered the Duke, "his Majesty sent no such message, but he would that you go with us to the home of her Grace, the Lady Elizabeth." The prince did not question a command that was so in accordance with his wishes, and they set off on horseback.

When the children were together, the duke bowed low before the boy of ten years, his own nephew, and said:—

"Your Majesty, graciously permit your faithful servants to kiss your hand and to promise you their humblest obedience both now and ever. A grievous duty is it, indeed, to declare to you that our illustrious king, Henry VIII., no more governs this realm of England. There is comfort for his sorrowing subjects in the thought that he has left us so noble and gracious a prince to rule us in his stead."

Edward had known nothing but kindness from his father, and now that the king was dead, Elizabeth no longer remembered what he had made her suffer. Edward forgot that he was a king, and the children threw themselves into each other's arms and sobbed and cried until those who were about them wept for sympathy.

Now the king had died three days before, but lest there should be some insurrection or an attempt to put Mary on the throne, the Duke of Somerset and others who meant to be the real rulers of the reign of Edward kept the news of his death a secret until they could get the young king safely into their hands and could establish the government in his name. Edward was conducted to the royal apartments in the Tower of London with an honorable escort of troops and nobles. There was great blowing of trumpets and waving of banners, and the boy was proclaimed king of England, France, and Ireland, and supreme head of the church in England and Ireland. A few weeks later the coronation took place, and then there was a rejoicing indeed. The streets through which the young king rode were hung with tapestry and banners. Here and there booths, or stages had been built, and in them all sorts of games and plays were carried on to amuse the people. A rope was stretched from the steeple of St. Paul's church and fastened firmly to a great anchor lying on the ground. An acrobat contrived to creep halfway up this rope, "aided neither by hand nor by foot," the old account says. Then he performed many feats in midair, "whereat," as the story puts it, "king and nobles had good pastime."

There was no longer a cruel king on the throne, but a child who is described as a marvel of goodness and learning. He is praised not only for his ability to speak different languages, but for his knowledge of geography. One of the historians of the day said that he could recite all the harbors and creeks in England, France, and Scotland, and could tell what kind of entrance there was in each for ships, and even which tides and winds were most favorable. It was claimed, too, that he knew the names of all the men of authority in his kingdom, where their homes were, and what their religion was.

This matter of religion was dividing the kingdom. Henry had called himself a Catholic, but he would not admit the Pope's authority. Edward and Elizabeth had been brought up in their father's belief. The Duke of Somerset was one of the men chosen to carry out Henry's will, and he was so decided a Protestant that he was almost as determined to make every one accept the Protestant faith as Henry had been to make all his people agree with himself. In spite of all King Henry's declarations that neither Mary nor Elizabeth should ever wear the crown, he had finally willed that it should descend first to Edward, then to Mary and then to Elizabeth. The Catholics were eager to have Mary come to the throne, because she was of their own faith; but the Duke of Somerset had been chosen Protector, that is, he was really to govern the kingdom until Edward was old enough to rule, and he meant to oblige the people to become Protestants.

There was even more scheming going on around the boy king, for his councilors were already planning for his marriage. A little five-year-old girl in Scotland was the one whose hand they meant to secure for their sovereign. Her name was Mary, and she was the Queen of Scots. This plan had been one of King Henry's favorite schemes, but it had never pleased the Scotch. The Protector led an army against them, a most remarkable fashion of winning a bride for the young king, but the Scotch would not yield.

"What greater honor do you expect for the queen?" demanded the English council. "How can Scotland gain more sure protection than that of the king of England?" The Scotch knew very well that if Edward married Mary, it would be for the purpose of gaining a surer control of Scotland, and they refused in spite of the Duke of Somerset and all his army. They betrothed the little queen to the son of the French king, and sent her to France to be educated. "The Scotch are a perverse and wilful people," then said the English.

Besides the difficulty in gaining a wife for the king and the religious persecutions, there was trouble from other causes, especially among the poor. Part of this arose from what was called "enclosing." On every great estate there had always been land that the poor people living on the estate could use as a common pasture for their cows. The rich landowners were beginning to "enclose," or fence in these tracts of land and to use them either for private parks or for sheep pastures. The poor had no longer any way to feed their animals, and they were in great distress. Somerset tried to forbid this enclosing, but the owners of land were too powerful for him, and the enclosing went on in spite of the strictest laws against it. Indeed, the laws caused a new difficulty, for now that the poor people had a decree in their favor, they revolted in several districts and tried to seize the land. A writer who lived in those times says, "The poor people swarmed in the realm."

Of course when there were revolts, Somerset was obliged to suppress them, no matter how much he sympathized with the revolters, and often accused men were punished with little effort to make sure of their guilt. It is said that a miller who had been a revolter suspected that he was in danger, and said to his servant, "I must go away on business. If anyone asks for me say that you are the miller and have owned the mill these three years. The king's officer came as the miller feared. "Are you the miller?" he demanded. "Surely," replied the servant proudly. "The mill has been mine for three full years." You have been a busy rebel," declared the officer, "and now you shall be hanged to the nearest tree." "Indeed, I'm not the miller, but only his man," cried the frightened servant. "The man tells two tales, hang him up," bade the officer. A little later one who knew the miller said, "Truly, he was not the miller, he was but the miller's man." "Then has he proved a good servant," declared the officer contentedly, "for how could he have done his master better service than by hanging for him?"

The nobles were angry at Somerset's attempt to prevent enclosing, and they were indignant that he should have so much power. The result was that he was accused of treason and the Duke of Northumberland became Protector.

Although all these acts were done in the name of Edward, the boy king had really very little freedom. "He is not alone half a quarter of an hour," said one who knew of his life. When he first became king, he wrote to Mary, "I will be to you a dearest brother and overflowing with all kindness;" but he was taught by Somerset and others that it was a danger to the kingdom to allow his sister to remain a Catholic. When he had been on the throne for about three years, she was summoned to court.

"Your Highness," said the chamberlain to Edward, "I have to announce the arrival of her Grace, the Princess Mary."

"Give welcome to her and her train," said the young monarch, "and say that it is my will and that of my councilors to receive her straightway." This visit was not for the pleasure of meeting her brother, though they greeted each other most cordially. The royal council was sitting in another room and there she was summoned.

"Your Grace," said the councilors, "is it true that, contrary to the wishes of his Majesty the king, mass is still said daily in your house?"

"It is true," answered Mary, "that the worship of God is carried on in my house in such wise as I do firmly believe is most pleasing to him."

"There is then no hope of your Grace's amendment shortly?"

"None, my lord."

"It is the will of his Majesty, who is supreme head of the church in England, that the mass should be no longer celebrated in his realm. It becomes the duty of all that owe him allegiance to obey. It is his Majesty's command that you obey as a subject, attempting not to rule as a sovereign."

"I will neither change my faith nor conceal that which is my true opinion," declared the princess, "and in testimony of my belief I am ready to lay my head upon the block for the truth, though I am unworthy to suffer death in so good a cause."

Mary soon left the palace. Letters bidding her give up her religion came from the king, but the elder sister replied:—

"They may be signed with your own name, but they cannot be really your own, for it is not possible that your Highness can at these years be a judge in matters of religion, and by the doings of certain of your councilors I mean not to rule my conscience."

With his councilors telling him how dangerous it was to the peace of the kingdom for Mary to be allowed to practise a form of religion that was contrary to the law, the brother and sister can hardly have been very happy together, and their meetings grew further apart.

Elizabeth was living quietly in her own house, spending most of her time in study. The boy king was hardly more than a toy in the hands of his councilors. Somerset was finally condemned to death, but when he wrote to Elizabeth and begged her to appeal to the king and save his life, Elizabeth was obliged to answer:—

"The king is surrounded by those who take good care to keep me away from him, and I can no more gain access to his Majesty than you can."

The one who was keeping Elizabeth from her brother was the new Protector, the Duke of Northumberland. Edward became ill, and everyone knew that his life would be short. Elizabeth tried to visit him, but was prevented. Then she wrote him a letter, but it is not probable that he ever saw it. Northumberland was in power, and he did not mean that either Mary or Elizabeth should wear the English crown; he had quite another plan in his mind.

CHAPTER IV

GIVING AWAY A KINGDOM

EDWARD was not fifteen when the Duke of Northumberland became Protector. At eighteen the boy king was to be really king and to govern his kingdom as he chose, but until then, although everything was done in his name, it was the Protector who would rule. Northumberland thought that in those three years he could gain so great an influence over the young sovereign that even when the time came to give up the high office, he would still retain much of his power.

Edward had never been strong, and before many months had passed, it was clear that he would not live to be eighteen. Northumberland had no mind to lose his power. What could he do?

One morning in June he went to the chamber of the king. Edward lay by the window looking out into the bright sunshine.

"My humble greeting to your gracious Majesty," said Northumberland. "I have brought news that cannot fail to give to your Highness an increase of health and strength."

"I think that nothing can do that," said Edward, "but good news will at least make the day less weary. What is it that you have to tell?"

"That two of those followers of the Pope who have most strongly opposed your Majesty's efforts for the good of the land have at last accepted godly counsel."

"I rejoice," said the king. "Would that the Princess Mary were one of them. Is it true, my lord, that no word of submission to him who is rightly the supreme head of the church in England has come from her Grace?"

"It is true, your Highness."

"Then when I die—no, my lord, do not deny it. I know well that few days are left to me—my sister will be on the throne. She will bring back the falseness of the old religion. Not the sovereign but the Pope will rule in the land, and I can do nothing to prevent it. How little power a king has!" Northumberland's heart beat fast. Now was his opportunity.

"Has your Majesty considered that the rightful heirs of king as well as of subject are those whom he himself shall name?"

"Do you mean, my lord, that it is my right to name her who shall follow me? that I could leave the crown to her Grace, the Princess Elizabeth, if I would?"

"Our glorious ruler, Henry VIII., bequeathed his crown as he would have it to descend. Surely, it would be in your Majesty's power to leave it to the

Princess Elizabeth's Grace or to whomever of the descendants of the illustrious sovereign, King Henry VIII., your Majesty might choose."

"The Princess Elizabeth was taught the principles of the truth even as I myself was," mused the king.

"True, your Majesty," agreed the duke, "but she is only twenty years of age. It might easily come to pass that she would wed a foreign prince of the false faith, and that the land, now so favored with the light of truth, would be again plunged into darkness. If she were already wed, it would be safer, though many in the realm believe that neither of the daughters of King Henry can rightfully inherit the crown. An heir upon whom all must unite would save strife and it may be bloodshed."

"That might well be," said the king thoughtfully. Then Northumberland suggested boldly, though with some inward fear:—

"The sisters of your Majesty's illustrious father, could you—" the duke hesitated.

"The granddaughter of Margaret Tudor is the Queen of Scots, the little maiden who refused my hand," said the king with a faint smile, "but she is of the false faith. The granddaughter of Mary Tudor is my old playmate, the lady Jane Grey, or is she not now Lady Dudley, my lord? Was it not a few days ago that she became the wife of your son? She is well-principled in the truth."

"Do not fancy, I beg your Highness, that a thought of what your Majesty had in mind moved me to look with favor upon the mutual affection of the young couple."

"No," said the young king a little wearily. "Arrange it in any way that you will to have the kingdom fall into the hands of her who will lead it more fully into the light, and bear it further from the idolatrous worship of the earlier days."

Northumberland had obtained his wish, but there must be lawyers to write a deed of gift of the crown. He went to three judges of the realm and gave them the king's command.

"Gladly would we see the faith of his Majesty more fully established," they said, "but, my lord duke, in the time of King Henry Parliament decreed that whoever did aught to change the order of succession to the crown should suffer death as a traitor."

Northumberland persuaded and threatened, but the judges had no mind to run the risk of losing their heads for the sake of setting his daughter-in-law upon the throne of England.

"If you had the written pardon of the king, would you do it?" demanded Northumberland, and after much discussion the judges hesitatingly agreed. Edward was now as eager as the Protector to have it made sure that Lady Jane would ascend the throne, and he willingly signed a pardon to free them from all punishment, if they were ever accused of breaking the law of the land. The pardon was signed, then the deed of gift, bequeathing the crown to Lady Jane, was signed. The dying king rejoiced, but the bold schemer trembled.

There were very good reasons why each of the four women had a right to feel honestly that she alone ought to be queen of England. These four were Mary, Elizabeth, Mary, the child Queen of Scots, who was descended from Margaret, sister of Henry VIII., and last, Lady Jane, who was descended from his youngest sister Mary. According to King Henry's will, which Parliament had confirmed, the crown was to go to Lady Jane, if Henry's three children died without heirs. It seemed quite possible that she might some day be the ruler of England, and her parents set to work to prepare her to become a queen.

Now when less than a century ago a lady in England found that her little daughter Victoria would probably be the sovereign of her country, she said, "I want you to be a good woman, and then I shall be sure that you will be a good queen." Lady Jane's parents thought more of training her to do everything according to the etiquette of the court, and they were so anxious that she should walk and talk and sit and eat and dance precisely as they thought a queen ought to perform those acts, that they were exceedingly severe with her. She was a gentle, loving girl, and she did her best to satisfy them, but she was upbraided and pinched and struck whenever she was in their presence. The one great pleasure in her life was the time that she spent with her teacher, whom she called "Master Aylmer," for he was so kind to her and so gentle in all his ways that she was happy when the hour of study had arrived.

Everyone knew that Northumberland was the most powerful man in the kingdom, and when he said to Lady Jane's father, the Marquis of Dorset, "If you will give your daughter to my son Guilford to wife, I will persuade the king to make you a duke," the marquis was delighted. Lady Jane was but sixteen and Lord Guilford Dudley was only one year older. They were married at once with the most brilliant festivities.

Not many days after the wedding, King Edward became very ill. "Hold yourself in readiness for what may be demanded of you," said Northumberland to Lady Jane. "Should the king fail to recover, you are made by his Majesty heir of his realm."

The girl of sixteen had never thought of such a thing as becoming queen of England until many years should have passed, and probably not even then, and she was greatly troubled. She dared not disobey Northumberland, and when a few days later he sent his daughter to bring her to the royal council, she did not venture to refuse. When the duke and the other members of the council entered the room, they fell on their knees before her and kissed her hand.

"We make our humble submission to your Majesty as our sovereign lady and rightful ruler of this realm of England," said they.

Lady Jane was much abashed, and she said:—

"My lords, I can but thank you for the grace that you show to one who is so unworthy of such honor; but if I understand your words aright, you greet me as your sovereign lady and ruler. My lords, there is surely some grievous error. His Majesty, King Edward, is, happily, still on the throne, and even if it had pleased God to remove his Grace from earth to heaven, no claim have I so long as the Princesses Mary and Elizabeth live. Will your lordships grant me permission to withdraw?"

Then spoke the Duke of Northumberland:—

"Your Majesty and members of the royal council, it is a painful duty that falls to my lot to announce the death of our beloved and illustrious king, Edward VI. Much reason have we to rejoice not only in his praiseworthy life and his countless acts of goodness and clemency, but especially in that he, being at the close of his days, thought most earnestly upon the welfare of his realm. In his last hour on earth he prayed that his kingdom might be defended from the popish faith, and he left it in the hands of her who he believed would be faithful to the trust, and would guard the land from falsehood and from error."

All her life Lady Jane had known and loved the young king. Tears came to her eyes. She looked pitifully about the room. Several noble ladies had been brought into the council chamber, but not one had even a glance of sympathy for the young girl. The Duchess of Northumberland frowned at her, and her own mother whispered sternly, "Demean yourself as is fitting for a queen."

"His Majesty gave command to his council," said the duke, "and they have no choice save to obey him. Thus declares the will of the king, signed and sealed, and drawn up by three capable judges of the realm. It names as his heir and successor on the throne of England her gracious Highness, Lady Jane, descendant of Mary, who was the youngest and most beloved sister of his Majesty, King Henry VIII."

Then all the lords of the council knelt at the feet of Lady Jane. "We render to your Majesty only the honor that is due," said they, "for you are of true and direct lineage heir to the crown. With deliberate mind we have promised to his Highness, King Edward VI., that in your Grace's cause we will spare neither goods nor lands nor the shedding of our blood."

Lady Jane stood before them, white and trembling. Then grief and pain overcame her, and with a sudden burst of tears she fell to the ground. When she was a little recovered, she said to them:—

"My lords, I can but grieve from my heart for the death of so noble a prince and one that was so dear to me. I am weak and feeble. I have little power to govern the land as he in his greatness of mind and of heart would have done, but if that which you say has been given me is rightfully and lawfully mine own, then will I turn to God in my insufficiency and humbly beseech his grace and spirit that I may rule the land to its advantage and to his glory and service."

In the afternoon of the same day Lady Jane went in state to the Tower of London, for it was an old custom that sovereigns should go forth from the Tower on the day of their coronation. Her relatives knelt before her and humbly promised to be obedient to her commands; and her own mother walked meekly behind her, bearing the daughter's train. In the evening she was proclaimed in London ruler of the kingdom.

Lady Jane Grey and Roger Ascham.—*From painting by J. C. Horsley*

There was little rejoicing. The people as a whole were sullen and silent, for most of them understood that the affair was but a scheme of Northumberland's to gain power for himself.

The duke knew that if Mary and Elizabeth were free after Edward's death was known, a party would be formed in favor of one or the other, and therefore he had planned to get them both into his hands. He sent messengers to them to say that the king was very ill and begged that they would give him the happiness and comfort of their presence.

Elizabeth paid no heed to the message. Either she was really ill, as she said, or she was wise enough to suspect that there was some trickery about this sudden demand for her society, when for so long a time she had not been allowed to see her brother. At any rate, she remained in her own house.

Mary returned word by a swift rider that she was made very happy by the thought that she could help to bring cheer and consolation to her brother, and she set out at once to go to him. When she was only a few miles from London, a man who had been her goldsmith came riding in hot haste.

"Your Grace," he said, "I beg that you will go no farther. The king is not ill, he is dead. Northumberland plans to set Lady Jane upon the throne. Flee, I do pray you." Mary hesitated. Was the word of the goldsmith true? Whom could she trust? Should she go on to London and perhaps be thrown into the prison of the Tower by Northumberland? Should she flee to Norfolk and refuse, it might be, her brother's last tender wishes? Was it a trap to make her declare herself queen and then behead her for treason? While she questioned, another rider came, a nobleman whom she trusted, and he told her that the king was indeed dead.

Mary turned toward Norfolk. Night came on. The princess herself and many of her retinue were exhausted. They asked for shelter at a country-seat. It was given them, but the Protestants in the neighborhood had heard that Edward was dead and that the Catholic princess was among them. A mob set out in the morning to destroy the house that had sheltered her. Mary had been warned of the danger and had ridden away. She glanced back from the top of a hill and saw the house in flames. "Let it go," she cried. "I will build him a better one."

As soon as she reached her own castle in Norfolk, she sent a letter to the royal council saying:—

"We are greatly surprised that we have had from you no knowledge of the death of our brother, but we trust your love and your loyalty. Whatever may have been said to us of any disloyal intentions on your part we do put far from us, and do agree to grant you pardon and receive you graciously into our service as true and faithful subjects."

Even though the councilors had failed to secure Mary, they still believed that their side would win, and they sent her a rather arrogant letter. It said:—

"Lady Jane is our queen, but if you will show yourself quiet and obedient as you ought, you will find us all ready to do you any service that we with duty may."

Mary then rode to Framlingham, a strongly fortified castle some twenty miles away. It was so near the sea that she could escape to the continent if flight should become necessary, but she could hardly have been in a safer place. The walls of the stronghold were eight feet thick; town and fortress were surrounded by three deep moats. Here she flung out her banner and called upon all loyal subjects to come to the assistance of their rightful queen. So many thousands gathered that she ventured to set out for London, and as she drew near the city, she met such a welcome that she disbanded her army.

Now at Edward's death when Northumberland saw that his plan to capture Elizabeth had failed, he sent a messenger to promise her land and money if she would but resign all title to the crown. With rare wisdom for so young a woman, she replied:—

"That is not for me to say. Lady Mary is by my father's will and by decree passed in open Parliament the rightful queen of the realm. Whatever my claim may be, I can make no challenge so long as my sister doth live." Elizabeth then set out to meet Mary, and, they entered London together, followed by a long train of ladies and noblemen, and escorted by the city guard.

Northumberland too, had collected an army, but his men deserted by hundreds. In less than two months after he had triumphantly set his daughter-in-law upon the throne, he was executed, together with two of those who had most strongly supported him. Lady Jane and her husband were imprisoned. Mary's advisers declared that there was no safety for her so long as Lady Jane lived, but Mary refused to put her to death.

As the day for the coronation drew near, there were great rejoicings. Many of those that did not wish to have a Catholic ruler were so glad to be free from Northumberland's schemes and to feel that she who was lawfully their queen was now on the throne that they were ready to unite in the joy of the others. In the procession to the Tower, Queen Mary rode in a litter, or chariot, drawn by six horses, glittering in their trappings of cloth of silver. She was robed in the richest of blue velvet, made even richer by bands of ermine. She wore a sort of head-dress, so heavy with gold and pearls and jewels that she often had to hold up her head with her hands. In a litter almost as splendid as her own rode Elizabeth and her first stepmother, Anne of Cleves. Noble ladies rode on horseback in all the splendors of crimson velvet. Companies of guards followed in white and green, the royal colors.

The next morning after all this magnificence, there was such a brilliant display as made the gorgeousness of the ride through the city seem simple and modest, for the queen was to be crowned in Westminster Abbey.

When she was on the platform in full view of the people, the Bishop of Winchester demanded of them whether it was their will that the crown should be placed on the head of the most excellent princess, Mary, eldest daughter of King Henry VIII. The people shouted, "Yea, yea! Queen Mary, Queen Mary!" Mary made a solemn promise to govern England aright and faithfully preserve the liberties of the people. Then followed all kinds of ceremonies, changing of robes, and sounding of trumpets. She was girded with a sword, a ring was put upon her finger, and at last the crown was solemnly placed upon her head. This was by no means the end of it all, for many nobles came to kneel before her and promise to be true to her. Each one of them kissed her cheek.

In all this ceremonial as well as in the feasting and the entertainments that followed it, the Princess Elizabeth was in every way ranked next to the queen. Elizabeth wore the coronet of a princess. "It is very heavy," she whispered to the French ambassador. "Be patient," murmured he, "it will be parent to a better one."

Parliament was soon in session, and one of the important questions to be decided was what should be done with Lady Jane.

"She attempted to seize the crown from Mary, who is our rightful sovereign," declared one, "and she should be put to death as a traitor."

"What she did was done at the bidding of the Duke of Northumberland," said another. "She was but a tool in his hands, and she should be freed."

"That cannot well be," objected a third. "Whoever commits a crime is guilty of that crime and must bear the punishment."

"Yes," agreed the first, "and moreover, some who would question Elizabeth's right to the throne would perchance unite under the banner of Jane. There will be neither rest nor safety in the kingdom so long as she is spared to lead any rebellious faction that may need a head."

Parliament decided that Lady Jane was guilty of treason, and she was sentenced to be either burned or beheaded as the queen should choose. Everyone was sorry for her. Even those that condemned her could hardly look upon the young girl without tears, and when she was taken back to her prison in the Tower, crowds of weeping people followed her.

"She is to be put to death 'at the queen's pleasure,' " said one royal attendant to another. "Do you believe it will be soon?"

"He who dwells in a palace should see but not speak," answered the other. "To you, however, I may venture to whisper that the death of Lady Jane will never be 'the queen's pleasure.' "

CHAPTER V

A PRINCESS IN PRISON

MARY did not forget to show gratitude to those who had aided her in gaining possession of her crown. To some she gave high positions, and for the one whose house had been burned she built a much finer residence.

"And now, my well-beloved cousin and councilor," she said to the Earl of Sussex, "we would gladly show to you our hearty appreciation of your loyalty in a troublous time. Ask what you will of us, and it shall be granted."

The only way of heating houses in those days was by means of fireplaces, and therefore, even the royal palaces were full of chills and drafts. Whenever the earl came to court, he took cold. A thought struck him and he said:—

"If your Grace is really of intent to bestow upon me the gift that will give me most of comfort and peace of mind and body, I would beg humbly for the royal permission that I need no longer uncover my head before man or woman."

Mary was greatly amused. "Either cap or coif or nightcap [skullcap] may you wear," said she, "and woe to the one that dares to dispute your privilege." The next morning a parchment bearing the royal arms was presented to the earl with all formality. It read:—

"Know ye that we do give to our well-beloved and trusty councilor, Henry, Earl of Sussex, license and pardon to wear his cap, coif, or night-cap, or any two of them, at his pleasure, as well in our presence as in the presence of any other person within this our realm."

Not all the questions of the day were settled as easily. One of the most important ones was who should succeed Mary on the throne. If she married and had children, they would be her heirs, but if not, the Princess Elizabeth would probably follow her as ruler of England. Now Mary was a strong and sincere Catholic, and her dearest wish was to lead England back to the old faith and have the Pope acknowledged as the head of the English church. She hoped to be able to bring this to pass, but she was not well, she had little reason to look for a long life, and when Elizabeth became queen, all Mary's work would be undone, the land would be again Protestant. Elizabeth was to Mary still the little sister whom she had so often led by the hand. Would it not be possible to persuade her to become a Catholic? Elizabeth had loved Edward, would she not go with Mary to hear a mass for the repose of his soul? Elizabeth refused. Again Mary asked, and again Elizabeth said no.

"She would not dare be so bold if stronger than herself were not behind her," declared Mary's councilors. "There is danger to life and throne in this audacity." Others too were to be feared, those Protestants who did not believe in the right of Elizabeth to the crown. They were not sorry to see disagreement between the two sisters, for if the younger should be shut out from the successsion, Lady Jane, prisoner in the Tower as she was, would be accepted as Mary's heir. Evidently Elizabeth must be induced to become a Catholic if it was possible. Mary begged and then she threatened. She had sermons preached before Elizabeth, and she sent the royal councilors to talk with her, but in vain. At last the princess was made to understand that she must yield or withdraw from court. More than this, it was said to her, "There are suspicions that you are bold in resisting the queen because you have support from without."

Elizabeth was alarmed, and she sent a message to the queen:—

"I pray you, let us meet, there is much that I would say." Soon the meeting came to pass. Mary entered the room attended by only one lady, who followed her at a greater distance than was customary. Elizabeth threw herself at Mary's feet and said with many tears:—

"Most gracious queen and sister, I have ever looked up to you with love and respect, and since I have had the use of my reason, I have been interested in everything that concerns your greatness and glory. It grieves me to the heart to feel that for some reason unknown to myself I am no longer as dear to your Majesty as I have believed myself to be."

"My well-beloved sister," answered the queen, "gladly would I show to you all affection if I were but sure that your heart was turned toward me and toward that which is not only my dearest wish but is for the salvation of your own soul."

"I have but followed the belief in which I was brought up," said Elizabeth. "Such books as my father approved have been my reading. I will study others if you will, and it may be that my mind will be opened to perceive truth in doctrines wherein I had not thought it to lie."

"It will be a pleasure to my chaplain to choose for you those that are of such quality as to lead a truly inquiring heart into the way of right."

"Yet another kindness do I beg of you, my queen and sister," said Elizabeth. "I have listened to those whom I was told to hear. Will your Grace send to me some well-taught preacher to instruct me in the way wherein you would have me to walk? Never have I heard any learned doctor discourse in such wise as to show me where lay my error." Mary agreed, and a few days later the two sisters attended mass together. Elizabeth even wrote to the German emperor that she intended to have a Catholic chapel opened in her own house, and asked his permission to purchase in Flanders a cross, chalice, and such ornaments as would be needed.

No one had much confidence in her sudden change of creed. Those Protestants who were discontented went on with their plots to make her queen, convinced none the less that once on the throne, she would restore the Protestant form of worship. The German emperor, who was Mary's chief adviser, urged that to insure the queen's safety Elizabeth ought to be imprisoned, or at any rate, so strictly guarded that she could do no harm. There was reason for his fears. Mary, Queen of Scots, would soon become the daughter-in-law of the French king, and while he was pretending to be a true friend to Elizabeth, he was in reality doing all in his power to make trouble between her and Mary. If Elizabeth could be led into some plot that would anger Mary and so could be shut out from the succession, his daughter-in-law might easily become queen of England as well as of Scotland. Vague rumors of discontent and plots came to the ears of Mary, and for some time she refused Elizabeth's request to be allowed to go to her own house.

The German emperor was Mary's cousin, Charles V., to whom she had been betrothed when she was a child. He was seventeen years older than she, and was the most powerful sovereign in Europe. To him she went for counsel concerning the difficult questions that pressed upon her. The most urgent one was that of her proposed marriage. She was to marry, that was settled, but the bridegroom had not yet been selected. No fewer than four foreign princes were suggested, but the English hoped most earnestly that she would marry an Englishman. Charles V. seemed to favor first one and then another, but he could always give good reasons why no one of them should be the chosen one. At last he named his own son Philip. Mary made many objections.

"The emperor is also king of Spain," said she to Charles's ambassador, "and when Philip succeeds him on the Spanish throne, how can he come and rule in England?"

"That matter would not be difficult to arrange," answered the ambassador. "The prince could rule in Spain and dwell in England, even as his father is able to rule both Spain and Germany."

"He is very young," said she.

"He is a staid man," declared the ambassador. "He has often had to stand in responsible positions, and indeed in appearance he is already many years older than your Majesty."

"When I marry, I shall marry as a woman, not as a queen," said Mary, "and I shall promise to obey my husband, but it will be my right to rule my kingdom. No foreigner may have part or lot in that. The English people would not bear it, nor would they endure to have places of honor or of power given to foreigners." Still, she did not reject Philip.

It was soon whispered about that there was a possibility of a Spanish marriage. The chancellor came to the queen and begged her to make no such alliance. "No other nation is so disliked as the Spaniards," said he, "and Philip's haughtiness and arrogance have disgusted his own subjects. Philip will rule the Low Countries, and the king of France will never endure it to have the Netherlands fall into the hands of England."

In spite of her objections Mary really favored the marriage with Philip. He was her cousin, of her own faith, and of her mother's nation. With Philip to support her, she could bring England back to the old faith. She allowed Charles's ambassador to discuss the matter again.

"Your Highness," said he, "never was a sovereign in a more difficult position. You stand alone without an honest adviser in the land. See how easily your councilors who were Protestants one year ago have now become Catholics. Will they not as readily become Protestants again, if they have good hope of farther advancement under the Princess Elizabeth? You are surrounded by enemies. There are those who do not love the true church, and there are the rebels who followed Northumberland; Lady Jane and the Princess Elizabeth stand ready for their hand. Then there are France and Scotland; the Scotch queen would willingly add England to her domain. In Spain lies your only hope."

"Even if what you say is true," she responded, "I am not a young girl whose hand is to be disposed of at the will of her father, I must see the prince before I decide."

"Pardon, your Majesty," said the ambassador, "but the emperor will never permit that his son and heir should be exhibited before the court as a candidate for your Majesty's hand, and perchance be rejected before the eyes of Europe. A man's face is a token of the man, shall a portrait of the prince be sent you?"

The queen agreed, and the picture was sent. It portrayed a young man with blue eyes, yellow hair and beard, and a rather gloomy expression; but the face must have pleased the queen, for when Parliament again begged her to marry none but an Englishman, it was too late. Two days earlier she had in the presence of the Spanish ambassador taken a solemn oath that she would wed no other man than Prince Philip of Spain.

Nothing was talked of in the kingdom but the Spanish marriage.

"It is a poor business," said one. "King Henry is but seven years dead, and his kingdom will soon be only a province of Spain."

"Not so fast," rejoined the other. "Spain is the richest country in Europe. I wish I had but the twentieth part of the gold that comes from the New World in one of those high-decked galleons of hers."

"For the queen to marry Philip will bring it no nearer to us," retorted the first.

"Why not, my friend? Will not freedom to trade help to fill our empty treasury? Spain is a strong ally. Let France and Scotland attack us, and it will be well to have a helper with ships and treasure."

"Ships and treasure will not give us freedom," declared the first. "Better be poor than be ruled by Spain. I'm as true a Catholic as you, but no wish have I to see the torture chamber of Spain brought into England. Philip's own subjects detest him."

Mary's councilors soon ceased to oppose what she so plainly wanted, though it was whispered about that they were convinced by bribes rather than by arguments. An ambassador came from Spain to bring the engagement ring and to draw up the marriage treaty. The English people were angry and indignant and the children played a game called "English and Spaniards." Philip was one of the characters in this play, and there was always a pretence of hanging him. Nevertheless, the treaty was drawn up. It was agreed that no Spaniards should hold office in England. If the queen should have children, they must not be carried out of the land without the consent of the nobles, and they should inherit not only England but the lands of Holland and Flanders to which Philip was heir.

In spite of all these careful arrangements, the English became more and more enraged, and there were insurrections in various parts of the country. One was headed by the Duke of Suffolk, Lady Jane's father. Mary had supposed that if Suffolk was forgiven and his daughter allowed to live, he would be loyal from gratitude, but this was not the case. He went from one place to another, raising troops and proclaiming Lady Jane queen of the realm.

Another insurrection was headed by a young poet named Wyatt. His forces came so near London that the queen was in great danger. Lawyers wore armor under their robes when they pleaded in court, and clergymen wore armor under their vestments when they preached. The insurgents came nearer, and there was hot fighting. "Flee, my queen, flee!" called one after another, but Mary was perfectly calm and answered, "I warrant we shall hear better news anon."

When it became clear that there would be bloodshed, Mary had written to Elizabeth, telling her of the danger and urging her to come where she would be protected. "Assuring you that you will be most heartily welcome," the letter ends. Elizabeth sent word that she was ill and not able to travel. Many days passed, and they were days full of events. The Duke of Suffolk was captured.

"You have pardoned him once," said Mary's councilors, "and his gratitude is but another attempt to thrust you from the throne. This time there can be no pardon." Mary agreed. "There is one thing more," said they. "There will be neither peace nor quiet nor safety in the land so long as Lady Jane lives."

"I can never sign the death-warrant of my cousin," declared Mary, "not even to save my own life."

"Have you a right to shed the blood of your subjects?" they demanded. "The ground about us is wet with their blood. Shall such scenes come to pass a second time?" Mary yielded, and Lady Jane was beheaded.

A question even more difficult than this had arisen. When Wyatt was examined, he declared that the Princess Elizabeth had known of the plot. Now Mary sent, not an affectionate invitation, but a command for her sister's presence. Two physicians accompanied the commissioners. They agreed that the princess was able to travel, and the company set out for the court. One hundred of her attendants escorted her, and one hundred more of Mary's guards followed. Elizabeth was greatly loved by the masses of the people. She was fine-looking, well educated, and witty, and they were proud of their princess.

"Draw aside the curtains," she commanded. "Let the people see me if they will." The people saw her indeed. Crowds lined the road as the procession moved slowly by.

"Alas, poor young lady," sobbed one kind-hearted woman. "I mind me well when her own mother went to the block."

"She's over young to be facing the cruel axe," declared another. "She's but the age of my own girl, only one and twenty, if she *is* a princess."

"Mayhap it will all be well," said a third. "See her sitting there in the fair white gown, and her face as white as the stuff itself. She's not the one to plot and plan to take the life of the queen."

Elizabeth came to the palace, but Mary refused to meet her.

"Bear this ring to her Majesty," commanded the princess. It was much the custom in those days for one friend to give another a ring whose sight should renew their friendship if misunderstanding had arisen between them, and Elizabeth wore one that had been given her by Mary long before. The pledge had lost its power, for Mary sent only the message, "Before we can meet, you must show your innocence of that of which you are accused."

Day after day it was debated what should be done with the princess. Although just before Wyatt's death he had taken back his words of accusation, the royal council still suspected her. Charles V. was more than willing that she should put to death, and the Spanish ambassador told Mary that until the punishment of the rebels had made the realm safe for Philip, he could not land on English soil. "It is most important," said he, "that the trial and execution of the Lady Elizabeth should take place before the arrival of the prince."

One morning ten of the royal commissioners demanded audience of Elizabeth.

"Your Grace," said the leader, "a grievous charge is made against you, that you were knowing to an evil and felonious attempt to overthrow the government and take the life of our most gracious queen. It is the pleasure of her Highness that you be at once removed to the Tower."

"I am an innocent woman," Elizabeth answered, "and I trust that her Majesty will be far more gracious than to commit to the Tower one who has never offended her in thought, word, or deed. I beg you to intercede for me with the queen."

The intercession was of no avail. Elizabeth sent a letter to Mary denying all charges and begging that they might meet, but the only reply was the order, "Your Grace must away to the Tower."

"I am content, inasmuch as it is the queen's pleasure," Elizabeth replied, and the carefully guarded boat set off. It drew up, not at the door which led to the royal apartments of the Tower, but at the one called the Traitors' Gate, where many a prisoner had been landed in the past troublous times.

"I am no traitor," said she, "nor will I go in at the Traitors' Gate."

"Madam, there is no choice," answered sternly one of the commissioners, but he added kindly, "The rain falls in torrents, will your Grace honor me by making use of my cloak?" Elizabeth flung it down angrily, and put her foot on the step, covered with water as it was.

"Here lands as true a subject as ever landed on these steps," she declared solemnly. Up the stairs she was taken, and to the room that was to become her prison. The doors were locked and bolted.

She was not without friends even within the walls of the Tower. Both Mary and Elizabeth were fond of children, and Elizabeth especially could always win their hearts. She had not been long a prisoner before one little girl, the child of an officer, began to watch for her when she walked in the garden.

"Lady," asked the child, "do you like to be in the Tower?"

"No, I do not," answered Elizabeth, "but the doors are locked and I have no key, so I cannot go out." In a few days the little girl came to her with a beaming face. "I want to tell you something," she whispered. "I want to tell it right into your ear." She threw her arms around the princess's neck and whispered: "I've brought you some keys so you needn't always stay here. Now you can open the gates and go out as you will, can't you?" and the child pulled from the bosom of her frock some little keys that she had found.

A boy of four years was one of her pets, and used to bring her flowers every day. The council suspected that he was bringing messages to her from another prisoner in the Tower and ordered his father to forbid his speaking to the princess. Nevertheless, the little fellow watched at the bolted door for a chance to say good-by, and called softly, "Lady, I can't bring you any flowers, and I can't come to see you any more."

In those times executions followed accusations so easily that Elizabeth was alarmed at every little commotion, and one day she asked anxiously whether the scaffold was still standing on which Lady Jane had been executed. The princess, was indeed, very near death at one time, for the queen's chancellor sent to the Tower an order for her execution. Mary was very ill and not expected to recover, and the chancellor may have thought that only the death of Elizabeth could save England for the Catholic church. The order was delivered to the keeper of the Tower.

"Where is the signature of the queen?" he demanded.

"The queen is too ill to sign the paper, but it is sent in her name."

"Then in her name will I wait until by the blessing of God her Majesty shall be well again, and can speak for herself," returned the keeper.

When Mary had recovered, she was exceedingly angry that the life of Elizabeth had been so nearly taken. It was soon decided that the princess should stay no longer in the Tower, but should be taken to the palace at Woodstock.

Elizabeth expected to be put to death. "Pray for me," she said to one of her servants, "for this night I think I must die." All along the way to Woodstock the people flocked to gaze upon her. They filled her litter with cakes and flowers and sweet-smelling herbs. Every one saluted her. "God save your Grace!" cried the crowds, and in one little village the bells rang a hearty welcome as she passed through. Nevertheless, she was a prisoner and as closely guarded as she had been in the Tower.

CHAPTER VI

FROM PRISON TO THRONE

WHILE one sister was in prison, the sister on the throne had not found life altogether happy. The more she gazed upon Philip's picture, the more she longed to meet him but he made no haste in coming. Two months had passed since Mary put on the betrothal ring, and never yet had he even written to her. Philip had begged his father to choose a young wife for him, but to the emperor the fact that Mary was ten years older than his son was a small matter if only he could secure for Philip a possibility of ruling England.

The marriage was to take place at Winchester, and as the time drew near, Mary set out with her retinue. She was borne in the royal litter, and if all the vehicles were as gorgeous as the one provided for her maids of honor, the procession must have been a dazzling sight. This one was a "wagon of timber work with wheels, axletrees, and benches." It was painted red, lined with red buckram, and covered with red cloth. This covering was adorned with heavy fringe of red silk.

Not at all agreeable was Philip's journey to Winchester. When he landed in England, he found a great company of nobles waiting to do him honor, and he was escorted to a palace in which most beautiful rooms had been prepared for him. This was pleasant, but when he set off for Winchester, the wind blew and the rain came down in floods, and the four or five thousand riders in the procession were thoroughly drenched.

Before they had ridden many minutes, a swift messenger drew rein in front of the prince, presented him a ring, and said:—

"Her Majesty the queen doth send your Grace this ring as a token that she would pray you to advance no farther."

Philip did not understand English perfectly. "There is danger," said he to his officers. "Little welcome have I from these English." It was explained to him that the queen's message only meant that she begged him not to expose himself to the storm, and he went on.

That evening the prince, all in black velvet and diamonds, made his first call on the woman whom he was to marry two days later. They talked together in Spanish for half an hour, and the next day they had another meeting, and Philip—now in black velvet and silver—stood with the queen under the canopy of state. She kissed him in greeting, and they talked together before the hundreds of ladies and nobles in the great audience hall.

On the following day came the marriage, and then there was such gleaming of pearls and blazing of rubies and flashing of diamonds as one might see in a splendid dream.

"Who giveth this woman to be married to this man?" asked the archbishop, and four great nobles of the kingdom came forward and answered, "We do give her in the name of the whole realm of England." A plain gold ring was put on the queen's finger, for "I will marry with a plain hoop of gold, like any other maiden," she had said. The people shouted, "God save our Queen! God send them joy!" and Mary of England had become the wife of Philip of Spain.

While the wedding rejoicings were going on, Elizabeth was a prisoner at Woodstock. What was to be done with her was the question. There was some reason to think that she had known of the plot to dethrone the queen, and in any case, if she was free, any leader of an insurrection could have an opportunity to try to win her support. Mary did not wish to keep her in the Tower, and she thought of sending her to some of her own Spanish relatives on the continent, but the royal marriage helped to decide the question, for Prince Philip expressed himself very decidedly to his royal wife that it would be best to set Elizabeth free.

"I would do it most gladly," said Mary, "could I be sure of her innocence."

"Does not your English law claim that one is innocent till he is proved guilty?"

"True," replied Mary, "but there is proof and there is no proof. My councilors declare that to set her free will be to say that she has been unjustly imprisoned."

"Can she not be induced to confess that she has done wrong and throw herself on your mercy?"

"Never," answered the queen quickly. "I have known her since she was a little child. When she storms and rages, she will yield, but when she quietly persists, she stands firm. I will see her. Nothing do I long for more than to believe that she is guiltless."

Elizabeth was sent for, and late one evening she had an audience with the queen. The younger sister knelt with her eyes full of tears and sobbed:—

"I beg your Majesty to believe in my truth and loyalty, no matter who shall say to the contrary."

"Then you will not confess," returned Mary. "You persist in declaring that you are innocent."

"If I am not innocent," said Elizabeth solemnly, "never again will I ask favor or kindness from the hands of your Grace."

"God knows," murmured the queen half turning away. A minute later she said, "Elizabeth, will you swear by all that you do hold sacred that you have no guilt in this matter?"

"I will," answered Elizabeth without a moment's hesitation.

"Then do I forgive you—be you innocent or be you guilty," she said to herself—"and in token of my pardon I restore to you the ring, pledge of my sisterly affection. May the time never come when you will have need to send it to me again."

At Christmas there was a grand round of festivities at court. The Pope had sent a representative to receive from Mary the humble submission of the kingdom, and the rejoicings were looked upon not only as celebrating this reconciliation but as in some measure continuing those of the queen's marriage. Elizabeth was made prominent in everything. She sat at the queen's table and was treated as heir to the throne. Nevertheless, Mary did not fully trust her, and when the princess was about to return to her own home, the queen presented a nobleman and said that henceforth he would abide in Elizabeth's house, charged with the duty of guarding her safety and comfort. This nobleman was a learned and upright man of most perfect courtesy, and his presence can hardly have failed to give her pleasure, even though Elizabeth well knew that he was sent to make sure that she had no connection with any of the plots which were to be feared.

It is no wonder that a close watch needed to be kept for conspiracies, for several were formed against the queen. A story was spread abroad that Edward VI. was not dead, but was living in France and was about to return to regain his throne. There were rumors that certain men in the land had the power of magic, and had stuck pins into waxen images of the queen, thereby causing her intense suffering. The king of France was ready to encourage any rumor, however absurd, and to aid any conspiracy that would better the chances of Mary of Scotland to wear the crown of England. If Elizabeth was dead or shut out of the succession, these chances would be greatly increased, and probably this is why Philip had now become the friend of Elizabeth, for if France and Scotland and England were united, his own power and that of his father would be much less. Several foreign husbands were proposed for the princess, one of them the son of Philip by a former marriage, a boy of ten years. Elizabeth refused them all, and the queen declared that she should not be forced to marry against her will.

Mary's reign was shamed and disgraced by the burning of a large number of persons, two hundred at least, because their religious belief differed from that which she thought right. She is called "Bloody Mary" because this took place in her reign, but just how far she was in fault no one knows. Neither Henry VIII. nor Edward nor Mary ever showed the least regard for the physical sufferings of others, but Mary had never manifested the least vindictiveness of disposition. Indeed, she had often been more inclined than her councilors thought best to pardon and overlook deeds that most rulers of the time would have punished. Moreover, during some of the worst persecutions Mary was so ill that it was said "she lay for weeks without speaking." One of the reasons why the English had feared to have Philip marry their queen, was because he was known to approve of torture, if by its means the sufferers could be induced to give up beliefs that he thought false. He now wrote to his sister, "We have made a law, I and the most illustrious queen, for the punishment of heretics and all enemies of Holy

Church; or rather, we have revived the old ordinances of the realm, which will serve this purpose very well." It must not be forgotten, however, that this burning at the stake was done with the consent of Parliament, and that, as Philip said, it was in accordance with the old laws.

A hard life was Mary's. She had no child, and she was not sure of the faithfulness of her sister and heir. It was chiefly by her determination to marry Philip that she had lost the love of her people, and after all that she had sacrificed for his sake and all her affection for him, he cared nothing whatever for her. An old ballad says that he liked

> "The baker's daughter in her russet gown
> Better than Queen Mary without her crown."

The crown of England was all that he cared for, and about a year after their marriage, he left very willingly for the continent. Mary controlled her sorrow at the public farewell, but as soon as that was over, she went to a window from which she could see Philip's barge, and there she sat with her head resting on her hands and wept bitterly till he was out of sight.

There was good reason why he should go, for his father wished to give him the sovereignty of the Low Countries; and there were some difficult questions that arose and prevented his immediate return. As months passed, Mary became more and more lonely. Her thoughts turned toward Elizabeth. Another plot had been discovered. Some of Elizabeth's own attendants were involved in it, and declarations were made that it was not unknown to the princess herself. Mary wrote her at once:—

"I pray that it may not seem to you amiss that it has been necessary to remove from your household certain dangerous persons, not the least of whose crimes it was that their confessions were but an attempt to involve your Grace in their evil designs. Rest assured that you are neither scorned nor hated, but rather loved and valued by me." With the letter went the gift of a valuable diamond.

After being away for nineteen months, Philip returned to England. Mary was so happy that she was ready to grant whatever he asked, though it was so great a boon as the aid of England in a war with France. Philip left in three or four months to carry on the war, and never again did his wife look upon the man whom she loved so well.

The war went on, and Calais, which had long been held by England, was taken by the French. The English were wrathful. Five hundred years earlier the kings of England had ruled wide-spreading lands in France. One had lost, another won, but never before had England been left without a foot of ground on the farther side of the Channel. Mary was crushed. "When I die," she said, "look upon my heart, and there you will see written the word 'Calais.'"

The summer of 1558 had come. Mary's thoughts turned more and more toward her sister. She left her palace and went to visit Elizabeth. She arranged a visit from Elizabeth to herself which was conducted with the greatest state. The princess made the journey in the queen's own barge with its awning of green silk beautifully embroidered. The queen's ladies followed her in six boats whose gorgeousness was almost dazzling, for the ladies were dressed in scarlet damask, in blue satin, and in cloth of silver, with many feathers and jewels. In the royal garden a pavilion had been built. It was in the shape of a strong castle, only the material was not gray stone, but crimson velvet and cloth of gold. The court feasted, the minstrels played, and the long, bright day came to its close.

Mary had never been well, almost every autumn she had suffered severely from sickness, and now a fever seized upon her. There was little hope of her recovery, but Philip sent her a ring and a message instead of coming to her. Parliament and the will of Henry VIII. had decided that Elizabeth should follow Mary as queen, but Philip begged Mary to name her sister as her heir in order to make the succession especially sure, and this was done. Mary grew weaker every day, the end must be near. The courtiers did not wait for it to come, crowds thronged the house of Elizabeth, every one eager to be among the first to pay his respects to her who would soon become their sovereign, and to assure her that, however others might have felt, he had never been otherwise than faithful to her and her alone.

Among these visitors was Count de Feria, one of Philip's train, who was in his master's confidence.

"My lord sends your Grace assurances of his most distinguished friendship," said the count. "He would have me say that his good will is as strong and his interest in your Grace's welfare so sincere as it was when by his influence, so gladly exerted, her Majesty was graciously pleased to release your Grace from imprisonment. He would also have me say that he has ever to the utmost of his power urged upon her Majesty that she should not fail to bequeath the crown to her only sister and rightful heir, and he rejoices that his words have had weight in her intentions."

"Most gracious thanks do I return to the king of Spain," answered Elizabeth, "and fully do I hold in my remembrance the favors shown to me in the time of my captivity. For all his efforts that I might be the heir of her Majesty, my sister, I return due gratitude, though verily I have ever thought myself entitled to the crown by the will of my father, the decree of Parliament, and the affection of the people."

Three or four days later Mary sent Elizabeth a casket containing jewels belonging to the crown and with it another casket of jewels belonging to Philip which he had given orders to have presented to her. Elizabeth well knew that the end of her sister's life could not be long delayed, and soon the word came that Mary was dead.

"It may be a plot," thought the wary princess, "to induce me to claim the crown while the queen lives, and so give my enemies a hold upon me. Sir Nicholas," she bade a faithful nobleman who she well knew had ever been true to her cause, "go you to the palace to one of the ladies of the bedchamber, the one in whom I do put most trust, and beg her that, if the queen is really dead, she will send me the ring of black enamel that her Majesty wore night and day, the one that King Philip gave her on their marriage."

Sir Nicholas set out on the short journey. The rumor had, indeed, preceded the death of the queen, but she died just as he reached the palace. Before he returned, several of Queen Mary's councilors made a hurried journey to Elizabeth's house at Hatfield.

"Your Highness," said they, "it is with the deepest sadness that we perform our duty to announce the death of her Majesty, Queen Mary. To your Grace, as our rightful sovereign, do we now proffer our homage, and promise to obey your Highness as the true and lawful ruler into whose hands the government of the realm has fallen."

Elizabeth sank upon her knees and repeated in Latin a sentence that was on the gold coins of the country, "It is the Lord's doing, and it is marvelous in our eyes."

Queen Mary died in the twilight of a November morning, but her death was not known at once in the city. Parliament was in session, and before noon the lord chancellor called the two houses together and said:—

"God this morning hath called to his mercy our late sovereign lady, Queen Mary; which hap, as it is most heavy and grievous to us, so have we no less cause, otherwise, to rejoice with praise to almighty God for leaving to us a true, lawful, and right inheritrix to the crown of this realm, which is the Lady Elizabeth, second daughter to our late sovereign of noble memory, Henry VIII."

For an instant there was silence, then the house rang with the cry, "God save Queen Elizabeth! Long may Queen Elizabeth reign over us!" The proclamation of her accession was now made in front of the palace of Westminster with many soundings of trumpets, and later, in the city of London.

"Did anyone ever see such a time?" said a Londoner to his friend at night. "No one would think that a queen had died since the day began; there has been nothing but bonfires and bell-ringing and feasting and shouting."

"When people are glad, their joy will reveal itself," answered his friend.

"There might well be reason for me to rejoice, but you are a Catholic, why should you welcome the Lady Elizabeth?"

"Is she Catholic or Protestant?" asked the other with a smile. "Who knows? There's one thing sure, she'll have a merry court, trade will be the gainer, and she'll marry no foreign prince."

"Perhaps having a new queen will also prevent another season of the plague and give us greater crops," laughed the first; and then he added more seriously, "Catholic or Protestant, I believe that there be few in the land who will not rejoice to see the death-fires no longer blaze at Smithfield."

A week later the queen rode from Hatfield to London. Hundreds of noble lords and ladies were in her retinue, and the number increased with every mile. The road was lined with people who shouted, "Queen Elizabeth! Queen Elizabeth! Long may she reign! God save the queen!" Children gazed at her eagerly, while their mothers wept tears of joy, and young men knelt and cried out their vows of loyalty and devotion. Many of the bishops of the realm came in a procession to greet her and begged to kiss her hand.

"Did you see that?" whispered a woman to her neighbor. "The queen wouldn't give her hand to the cruel bishop of London. She knows well it's because of him that more than one good man's been burned at the stake. Oh, but she'll be a good queen, God bless her!"

The lord mayor and the aldermen came in their scarlet robes to escort her to the palace, and a few days later she went in state to the Tower of London. The streets were strewn with fine gravel, rich tapestries adorned the walls, banners waved, trumpets sounded, boys from St. Paul's school made Latin speeches in her praise, and great companies of children sang joyful songs of welcome.

Elizabeth looked very handsome as she rode into the city on horseback, wearing a habit of the richest purple velvet. She replied to everyone's greeting, and made little Latin speeches in answer to those of the schoolboys. At last she came to the Tower, and this time she entered, not at the Traitors' Gate, but through the royal entrance, and passed between long lines of soldiers, drawn up, not to keep watch over a prisoner, but to do honor to a queen.

CHAPTER VII

A SIXTEENTH CENTURY CORONATION

THERE were several matters concerning which the English people were eagerly watching to see what the queen would do, but whether her subjects expected to be pleased or displeased with her deeds, they could hardly help looking forward with interest to the grand ceremonial of the coronation. Astrology was in vogue, and every nobleman who wished to be in fashion had his horoscope drawn up. When a soldier was setting out for war or a captain was embarking on some dangerous voyage, he would go to a reader of the heavens to be told on which day he must start in order to have his expedition result prosperously. Queen Elizabeth was a firm believer in the foretelling of destiny by the stars, and she had especial confidence in an astrologer called Dr. Dee. To him, therefore, she went that he might name a fortunate day for the coronation. He named Sunday, January 15, 1559.

It was the custom for the sovereigns to ride through the city of London in great state on their way to Westminster, where they were crowned, and Elizabeth's ride was one of the most brilliant ever known. There were trumpeters and heralds in glittering armor; there were ladies on horseback in habits of crimson velvet; there were nobles in silks and satins and laces, gleaming with gold and sparkling with jewels; there were long lines of guards in the green and white of the Tudors; and in the midst of all the splendor was the queen in a gorgeous chariot lined with the richest crimson velvet.

She bowed, she smiled, she waved her hand, she leaned to one side of her carriage and then to the other and listened intently to whatever any one wished to say to her, and whether it was the lord chancellor or the poorest woman in London, each one was sure of a pleasant word and a gracious smile from this new sovereign. Gifts were showered upon her. The city of London gave her a crimson satin purse filled with gold and so large that she had to take both hands to lift it. Elizabeth thanked the citizens and said:—

"To honor my passage through the town you have been at great expense of treasure, so will I spend not only treasure but the dearest drops of my blood, if need be, for the happiness of my people."

"Your Grace," said a poor woman in humble garb, "I could bring you only this bit of rosemary, but there's many a blessing goes with it."

"I thank you heartily," responded the queen. "It shall go with me to Westminster," and it did.

"I can remember fifty years ago when old King Harry was crowned," a white-haired man called to her.

The queen smiled upon him. "May you live to remember me as long," she responded. Then she bade her chariot be stopped. "I wish to hear what the child is saying," she said, for a pretty little boy was reciting some verses in her praise. "Turn to one side so I can see his face."

Over several of the streets great arches had been built with various exhibitions called pageants. One represented a cave, and from it Time was leading forth his daughter Truth. The young girl who took the part of Truth held in her hand a most beautifully bound English Bible.

"Who is that with the scythe and hourglass?" the queen asked.

"Time," was the answer.

"It is time that has brought me here," she said as if to herself. The chariot moved slowly on, and when it was almost under the arch, "Truth" let down the volume by a silken cord. Elizabeth took the Bible, kissed it and pressed it to her heart, then held it up before the people.

"Truly, I thank my city of London," said she. "No other gift could have pleased me as this does, and I promise you that every day I will read it most diligently."

So it was that Elizabeth made her journey through London. The whole scene was rather theatrical, but it pleased the people, and that was what she most wished to do. All around her were shouts of joy, silent tears of happiness, wild promises of service, and sober, heartfelt prayers. As she came to the gates of the city, she looked back and called, "Farewell, my people, farewell. Be well assured that I will be a good queen to you." Then the cannon of the Tower thundered, and Elizabeth went on to Westminster.

There she was crowned, and Sir Edward Dymock performed the office of champion, introduced by William the Conqueror. At the coronation banquet he rode into the hall in full armor, threw down his gauntlet and proclaimed:—

"If there be any manner of man that will say and maintain that our sovereign lady, Queen Elizabeth, is not the rightful and undoubted inheritrix to the imperial crown of this realm of England, I say he lieth like a false traitor, and *that* I am ready to maintain with him, and therefore I cast him my gage." After a few minutes a herald picked up the glove and presented it to Sir Edward. This ceremony was repeated at two other places in the hall. The queen then drank to the health of the champion in a golden cup which was presented to him as his reward.

During the glories of the coronation, the people seemed to have almost forgotten for a moment the important question whether the queen would rule as a Catholic or a Protestant. There had been much discussion about the matter, and after the days of celebration there was even more.

"She was brought up as a Protestant," one man said, "and she will rule as a Protestant."

"Oh, but has she not declared that she is a Catholic, and has she not been to mass with Queen Mary? Does she not go to mass now?" retorted another.

"Who wouldn't go to mass to gain a kingdom?" laughed a third lightly. "If Queen Mary had named the queen of Scotland as her heir—yes, I know there was a decree of Parliament, but another decree might have been passed as well as that—I don't say the Catholics would have tried to make the Scotch girl queen, but Elizabeth was wise, she was wise."

"It is two full months since Queen Mary died," said the second thoughtfully, "mass is said in the churches every day. Her Majesty will have no preaching without special permission, but———"

"No wonder," broke in the third, "after the sermon that the bishop of Winchester preached at Queen Mary's funeral. He praised Mary to the skies, then said she had left a sister whom they were bound to obey, for 'a live dog is better than a dead lion.' A preacher will have to hide his thoughts in something deeper than Latin to keep them from the queen. I don't wonder that she looks after the sermons."

"I know that she has been to mass many times since Mary died," admitted the first, "but don't you know what she did on Christmas morning? She went to church with her ladies and she heard the Gospel and the Epistle, but before the mass she rose all of a sudden and left the chapel. No true Catholic would stay away from mass on Christmas day."

"She might have been ill," suggested the second.

"As ill as she was when Queen Mary sent for her to come and prove that she had nothing to do with Wyatt's rebellion," said the third drily. "Now mark my words, Elizabeth, queen of England, will never journey by a path because it is straight; she'll keep two roads open, and she'll walk in the one that has the best traveling."

This uncertainty about Elizabeth's religious ideas was one reason why she was welcomed to the throne so warmly. By birth and training she was a Protestant, and therefore no Protestant could consistently oppose her. In her later years she had declared herself a Catholic, and the Catholics had a reasonable hope that she would show favor to them. Another good reason was that there was neither Protestant nor Catholic who could have been set up against her with strong probability of success. Mary of Scotland was the next heir, and she was a Catholic, but no loyal Englishman, no matter what was his creed, wished to see the queen of France raised to the throne of England.

Elizabeth was twenty-five when she became queen, and in her quiet years of study and observation she had formed two very definite ideas about ruling the kingdom. She meant to hold the power in her own hands over church as well as state, and she meant to use her mastery for the gain of the people. Her father had claimed this authority and had exercised it; while Edward reigned, certain noblemen had ruled; while Mary reigned, the church had ruled. Elizabeth wished to be supported by nobles and church if possible, but her chief dependence was upon the masses of people. When she made her first speech to judges of the realm, she said: "Have a care over my people. They are *my* people. Every man oppresseth and despoileth them without mercy. They cannot revenge their quarrel nor help themselves. See unto them, see unto them, for they are my charge." When Elizabeth was in earnest and really meant what she said, she generally used short, clear sentences whose meaning could not be mistaken; but when she had something to hide, she used long, intricate expressions, so confused that they would sometimes bear two opposite interpretations, and no one could declare positively what she really meant to say.

This determination of hers to win the support of the people was chiefly why she did not hasten to make sudden changes in the church. She did not at once object to saying mass, but she ordered the Gospel and the Epistle to be read in English as in the Protestant church. Then before she went any further she waited to meet her Parliament and see whether this change had aroused opposition.

She had chosen for her chief adviser Sir William Cecil, afterwards called Lord Burleigh. He was a man of great ability and a Protestant, though he had never shown any desire to become a martyr for his faith. He held a high position during Edward's reign, but while Mary was in power, although he went to mass as the law required, he had little to say about church matters. He lived quietly on his estate, interested in his fawns and calves, writing letters about the care of his fruit trees and about buying sheep; but during these quiet years, he was reading and thinking and planning, and gaining wisdom in all that pertained to ruling a land.

When Elizabeth made him her secretary, she bade him always tell her frankly what he believed was best, whether he thought it would please her or not. He wished to reestablish Protestantism, and before Elizabeth had been on the throne five months, a decree was passed that she and not the Pope was supreme governor of the church in England. To dispute this decree was declared to be treason, but only clergymen and those who held office under the crown were obliged to take the oath. A man who refused was not beheaded as in Henry's day, but he was put out of his office, and according to the ideas of times, that was not a severe penalty for such an offence. The Catholic form of worship was forbidden, and, while no one not in office was obliged to tell his belief, all subjects were commanded to attend the Protestant service or pay a fine.

Elizabeth did not go as far as this without watching closely for hints of what the majority of her people were willing to permit. One hint came to her the morning after her coronation. She had freed a number of prisoners, as was the custom at the crowning of a sovereign, and after the act one of her courtiers knelt at her feet with a roll of parchment in his hand and said:—

"Your Majesty, will you graciously lend ear to an earnest request from many of your subjects?"

"To do for my beloved people that which is for their good will ever be the ruling desire of my heart," replied the queen.

"Then do I humbly beg in the name of all these good subjects and true"—and he unrolled the parchment to show the long list of signatures—"I beg that your Highness will release unto us yet four more prisoners."

"And who may these prisoners be that have won so zealous an advocate?" asked the queen.

"Verily, your Grace, their names be Matthew, Mark, Luke, and John. They have been shut up in a language not understanded of the people, as if they were in prison. Even to a prisoner speech with his friends is not often forbidden. Will your Majesty graciously command that the words of the four Evangelists be put into English that these captives may be released from their dungeon?" This was really asking whether she would rule as a Protestant, for the Catholics opposed the circulation of the English Bible.

The queen showed no displeasure, but answered with a smile:—

"It has sometimes come to pass that men have learned to prefer their prison. Perchance it would be better to inquire of these prisoners of ours whether they wish to come out from behind the bars." When Parliament met, the question was brought up, and a translation of the Bible was ordered to be made at once. This was issued as authorized by the queen.

There was another matter that perhaps weighed more seriously upon the masses of the people than did the question which form of religion the queen would favor, and that was her marriage. The English longed to feel sure that the government would go on peacefully even if their queen should be taken from them. Before Henry's father came to the throne, there had been in England a terrible time of civil war because there were different claimants to the crown who were supported by different parties, and most people in the land would rather have a form of worship with which they did not agree than feel that the death of their sovereign would be followed by a return of those bloody days. If Elizabeth married and had a child to inherit the crown, the land would settle down to quiet.

This was the way King Philip reasoned as well as the English. Then he thought: "Elizabeth is a wise, shrewd woman, and she can see that with France and Scotland against her, her only hope is to ally herself with Spain. The only way to be sure of Spain's support is to marry me or some true friend of mine." As for her Protestantism, he did not think that matter of any great importance, for he believed that she would rather be sure of her throne than of her church.

When Elizabeth became queen, she had sent, as was the custom, a letter to the various rulers of Europe, formally announcing her accession. Philip's plans were made before the letter reached him. He had concluded that his only safe course was to marry her himself. He wrote to his ambassador, Count de Feria, and explained why he had come to such a conclusion. It was a great sacrifice, he said, for it would not be easy to rule England in addition to his other domains, and Elizabeth must not be so unreasonable as to expect him to spend much of his time with her. She must give up her Protestant notions, of course, become a Catholic, and agree to uphold the Catholic faith in her country. To marry the sister of his dead wife was against the

law of the church, but he was sure that he could induce the Pope to grant special permission.

Philip's reply to Elizabeth's announcement was
an ardent letter begging her in most eloquent terms to
become his wife. The queen met his request with the
gravest courtesy, thanked him for the honor that he
had done her, and told him how fully she realized of
what advantage such a splendid alliance would be to
her. Philip wrote again and again; he told her how
highly he thought of her abilities and merits, and what
a charming, fascinating woman she was. Elizabeth was
shrewd enough to understand why this keen politician
was so eager for the marriage, but she answered his letters with the utmost politeness, and when other excuses failed, she told him that she could not make any
plans concerning marriage without consulting Parliament, and that body was not yet in session. She mis-
chievously allowed her ladies to see his glowing
epistles, but perhaps she may be pardoned for this offence, inasmuch as Count de Feria had foolishly shown
the king's letter, and Elizabeth knew precisely what
Philip had said about the great sacrifice he was making
in wedding her. Philip was so sure she would marry
him that he sent envoys to Rome to get the Pope's
permission, but before they could return, a final letter
came from the queen, refusing to take him for her
husband. The Spaniard was easily consoled, for within
a month he married the daughter of the French king.

How much attention the queen proposed to pay
to the advice of Parliament in this matter was seen a
little later when the House of Commons sent a delega-
tion to her, begging that they might have the great

honor of an interview with her Majesty. Elizabeth put on her royal robes and went to the House in all state. An address was made her. The speaker told her how they gloried in her eminence and rejoiced in having her for queen. Then he laid before her the affliction it would be to the land if she should die and leave no child to inherit not only her crown but her goodness and her greatness. Finally he begged in all humility that she would in her own good time choose among her many suitors the one most pleasing to herself.

Elizabeth was silent for a moment, and the House feared that she might be offended, then she smiled graciously and thanked them most heartily for their love of her and for their care of the kingdom. "I like your speech," she said, "because it does not attempt to bind my choice; but it would have been a great presumption if you had taken it upon yourselves to direct or limit me whom you are bound to obey." She told them that whatever husband she chose should be of such character that he would care for the kingdom even as she herself did. Finally she said that if she did not marry, they ought not to feel anxious about the realm, but to trust in God, for in due time he would make it evident into whose hands he wished the kingdom to fall. Then she left the House, smiling so pleasantly and bowing so graciously that few among them realized at once that she had neither agreed with them nor disagreed, and that she had promised them nothing at all. She had merely declared that she intended to have her own way and that they had nothing to say about the matter.

King Philip was by no means the only man who was eager for the hand of the English queen. There was Philip's friend, the Archduke Charles, there were two French princes, the king of Sweden, the king of Denmark, the king of Poland, the Scotch Earl Arran, the English Earl of Arundel, and still others as the months passed. Several of these ardent wooers sent envoys to England to plead their cause; the king of Sweden sent his brother, and the king of Denmark straightaway despatched his nephew on the same errand. These agents were received with the highest honors, entertainments were arranged for their pleasure, and every courtesy was shown them. Elizabeth was graciousness itself to each, and made each believe that she was especially inclined to favor his master, but that for reasons of state she could not give an answer at once. So she kept them waiting for her royal decision, playing one against another, and all this time England was growing stronger.

Whether she was in earnest when she declared that she did not wish to marry, no one knows, but many think that her final refusal to one suitor after another was because the only man for whom she cared was Robert Dudley, Earl of Leicester, son of the Duke of Northumberland. He was a man without special talent or ability, a handsome courtier with graceful manners and much ambition. He was married to Amy Robsart, a beautiful girl and a great heiress, but while he was at court, she was left in a lonely mansion in the care of one of Leicester's dependents, a man who had the reputation of being ready to commit any crime for which he was paid. Two years after Elizabeth's accession, Amy Robsart was found dead at the foot of a staircase, and many believed that she had been murdered. They would have believed it still more firmly if they had known that a very short time later Leicester was trying to persuade Philip that he would protect the Catholics if he could be aided to marry the queen, and to convince the French Protestants that he would do the same for their church if he could have their help in winning the hand of Elizabeth. As for the queen herself, she would at one time show the earl every sign of tenderness, and at another she would declare, "I'll marry no subject. Marry a subject and make him king? Never."

CHAPTER VIII

A QUEEN'S TROUBLES

NEVER had a queen a greater variety of difficulties to meet. If she favored the Catholics, the Protestants would not support her; the Puritans were beginning to be of some importance, and they were eager to have every trace of Catholicism destroyed; but if she introduced Protestant changes too rapidly, the Catholics might revolt. She wished, it is probable, to refuse her numerous suitors, but she needed to keep on friendly terms with each as far as possible. The royal treasury was low, and among the nations of Europe there was not one upon whose assistance England could count in case of need.

Such were Elizabeth's troubles at the beginning of her reign, and as the months passed, the difficulties became even more complicated. Scotland was ruled by Mary's mother, who acted as regent for her daughter. She was French and a Catholic, and as more and more of the Scotch became Protestants, they were determined to have freedom for Protestant worship. Persecution followed, imprisonment, torture, and burning at the stake. Then came a fierce revolt. By the aid of

France this was suppressed, but the Protestants appealed to Elizabeth.

"No war, my lords, no war," declared she to her council. "A queen does not lend aid to rebels."

"The rebels are in a fair way to become the government," suggested one councilor.

"England cannot afford war," declared another. "We have no money to spend on fleets and armies."

"The French are already in Scotland," said one. "More will follow, and their next step will be across the border. If they are once in England, we shall have to raise armies whether we can or not."

"True," agreed another, "and surely it is better to fight them in Scotland than on our own soil."

"If we attack the French, Philip will aid them and try to put Mary on our throne."

"No, no," shouted three or four voices. "To unite France, Scotland, and England under one ruler would weaken his own power. He'll not do that."

"This is a question of religion as well as policy," said another. "Shall not the government of the church of England aid the Protestants of Scotland?"

This last argument did not count for very much with Elizabeth, but there was another one that did. She left the council and thought over the matter carefully and anxiously. "If I can get power in Scotland," she said to herself, "I can induce the Scotch government to agree that Mary shall never claim the title of queen of England." Money was borrowed from Antwerp, and England began to prepare for fighting.

France became uneasy and sent word to Elizabeth:—

"We do protest and remonstrate against the ruler of a neighboring kingdom giving aid to rebels and revolters." The French well knew how sorely aggrieved the English felt at the loss of Calais, and as a bribe to the queen they offered to give her back the town and citadel if she would agree not to aid the Scotch Protestants.

Elizabeth knew then that the French feared her, and she replied:—

"So long as the Queen of Scots doth falsely claim to be also queen of this my realm, then so long must I guard myself in the way that seems to me wisest and best. To free my throne from the attacks of false claimants and so secure peace and safety for my people is worth far more to me than any little fishing village in a foreign country."

The French were driven from Scotland, and a treaty was made agreeing that Mary should give up all claim to the throne of England. Mary had empowered her agents to make whatever terms they thought best, but when she saw this provision she refused to sign the treaty.

One year later a beautiful young woman stood at the stern of a vessel, looking back with tearful eyes at the shore from which she had sailed. The twilight deepened, and night settled around her. She turned away. "Adieu, my beloved France," she whispered, "farewell, farewell."

Thus it was that a queen returned to her kingdom, for the fair young woman was Mary, Queen of Scots. Her husband had died, and there was no longer any place in France for her. Scotland asked her to return to the throne that had been her own ever since she was a few days old. She was only nineteen, and she was leaving the gay, merry court in which nearly all her life had been spent; she was leaving her friends and companions, and for what? Scotland was the land of her birth, but it was a foreign country to her. It was not like her sunny France, it was a land of mist and of cold, of plain habits and stern morals. The queen was coming to her own, but her own was strange to her.

Mary had asked Elizabeth's permission to shorten the voyage by passing through England. "That must not be," thought the English queen. "Her presence here would be the signal for all the discontented Catholics in the kingdom to follow her banner." Permission was refused, unless Mary would agree beforehand to give up all claim to the English crown.

"I ask but Elizabeth's friendship," said Mary. "I do not trouble her state nor try to win over her subjects, though I do know there be some in her realm that are not unready to hear offers"—but she would not promise to give up her claim to the crown. She was fully as independent as Elizabeth, and she added regretfully, "I grieve that I so far forgot myself as to ask a favor that I needed not. Surely, I may go home into my own realm without her passport or license. I came hither safely, and I may have means to return."

Scotland rejoiced that the queen had come, and welcomed her with bonfires and music and speeches of welcome. The Scotch supposed that they were pleasing her, but Mary wrote to her friends:—

"In Edinburgh when I would have slept, five or six hundred ragamuffins saluted me with wretched fiddles and little rebecks, and then they sang psalms loudly and discordantly; but one must have patience."

No one can help feeling sympathy with the lonely girl of nineteen who had left all that she loved to come and rule over a country that seemed to her almost barbarous in contrast with her beloved France. She was a Catholic; most of her people were Protestants. She won many friends and admirers, but she never gained the confidence and steady affection of her people that made Elizabeth strong. The queen and her subjects grew further apart. Mary had been brought up to believe that the marriage of Anne Boleyn was not lawful, and that therefore she herself and not Elizabeth was the rightful queen of England. The French king had taught her to sign herself "Queen of Scotland and England." Now that she had returned to Scotland, she dropped the latter part of the title, but demanded that Elizabeth should declare her heir to the throne, as she certainly was by all laws of the hereditary descent of the crown. Elizabeth firmly refused.

It was probable that Mary would marry, and it was a matter of importance to Elizabeth that the husband should not be one who could strengthen the

Scotch claim to the throne. Mary consulted Elizabeth about one or two of her suitors, and suddenly the English queen surprised all Europe by offering to Mary the unwilling hand of her own favorite, the Earl of Leicester, and hinted, though in her usual equivocal fashion, that if Mary would marry the earl, she would be recognized as the next heir to the crown. "I would marry Robin myself," declared the queen to Mary's commissioner, Sir James Melville, "save that I am determined to wed no man."

Elizabeth talked with Sir James most familiarly, and this woman who was so shrewdly guiding her millions of Englishmen and guarding her throne from Mary of Scotland, often seemed to think of nothing but whether she or her rival had the prettier face.

"Which is the fairer?" she demanded, "I or the queen of Scotland?"

"Your Majesty is the fairest queen in England, and ours is the fairest queen in Scotland," replied Sir James wisely.

"That is not an answer," declared Elizabeth. "Which of us two is the fairer?"

"Your Majesty is whiter, but our queen is very winsome."

"Which is of greater stature?"

"Our queen," replied Sir James.

"Your queen is over high then," said Elizabeth, "for I am neither too high nor too low. But tell me, how does she amuse herself?"

"She hunts and reads and sometimes she plays on the lute and the virginals."

"Does she play well?"

"Reasonably well for a queen," declared Sir James audaciously.

"I wish I could see her," said Elizabeth.

"If your Grace should command me, I could convey you to Scotland in the dress of a page, and none be the wiser," suggested Sir James gravely, and Elizabeth did not seem at all displeased with the familiarity.

When the commissioner was again in Scotland, Mary asked what he thought of Elizabeth. "She has neither plain dealing nor upright meaning," said he, "and she is much afraid that your Highness's princely qualities will drive her from her kingdom."

Leicester was refused. Mary was now twenty-three, but she chose for her husband Lord Darnley, a handsome, spoiled child of nineteen. He was a Catholic and after herself the next heir to the English throne. Elizabeth was angry, but she was helpless.

A year later Sir James made a journey from Scotland to London in four days, as rapid traveling as was possible at that time. He called upon Lord Burleigh and gave him an important message. It was evening, and the queen was dancing merrily with her ladies and nobles when Cecil whispered a word in her ear. No more mirth did she show. She sat down, resting her head on her hand. The ladies pressed around her. Suddenly she burst out, "The Queen of Scots has a fair young son, and I am but a barren stock."

When Elizabeth found that it was impossible to have her own way, she usually accepted the situation gracefully. Sir James came to see her in the morning. She met him with a "volt," a bit of an old Italian dance, and declared the news was so welcome that it had cured her of a fifteen-days' illness. She agreed to be godmother to Mary's son, and as a christening gift she sent a font of pure gold.

The next news from Scotland was that Lord Darnley had been murdered, and that there was reason for believing the Earl of Bothwell, a bold, reckless adventurer, to have been the murderer. Mary had soon tired of the silly, arbitrary boy and had kept her dislike no secret. Two months later she married Bothwell, and there were so many reasons for thinking that she had helped to plan the murder that the Scotch nobles took up arms against her, and imprisoned her in Lochleven Castle, until she could be tried. She was forced to sign a paper giving up all claim to the Scotch throne, and her baby son James, only one year old, was crowned king of Scotland.

Elizabeth raged that mere subjects should venture to accuse a queen as if she were an ordinary person. "How dare they call their sovereign to account?" demanded the angry ruler of England. She declared that Mary's throne should be restored to her and that the rebels should be punished. Indeed, in her wrath she made all sorts of wild vows and threats which she had no power to keep.

This support, however, encouraged Mary's friends to attempt her rescue. She escaped from Lochleven; her followers fought an unsuccessful battle; she rode on horseback, sixty miles in a single day; she was taken in a fishing boat to the English side of Solway Frith; and then the deposed queen was safe in England, in the realm of the sovereign from whom she believed she might expect assistance.

Elizabeth and her council considered the matter long and earnestly.

"Let us return her to Scotland."

"Then she will be put to death, and the Catholics of Scotland and England will be aroused against Queen Elizabeth."

"Shall we place her back upon the Scotch throne?"

"We could not without war with Scotland and probably with France."

"Shall we invite her to remain in England as the guest of the queen?"

"And offer her as a head for every conspiracy that may be formed against her Majesty? No."

"There is something else. We have a right to know whether we are protecting an innocent young woman who had fled to us for help, or a criminal who has aided in the murder of her husband."

So the question was discussed, and it was finally decided that Mary should be kept as a prisoner and tried before special commissioners appointed for the purpose. At the end of this investigation Elizabeth declared that she had been proved neither innocent nor guilty. That question was dropped, but in spite of her angry protest and her demands to be set free, the queen of Scotland was kept in England for eighteen years, treated in many respects with the deference due to a sovereign, but guarded as closely as any prisoner.

In the midst of these complications that required the keenest acumen of the most vigorous intellect, Elizabeth did not lay aside her whims and vanities. One of her favorite customs was that of wearing an "impress," a device somewhat like a coat of arms, which was changed as often as the wearer chose. Each "impress" had a motto, and the queen used a different one almost every day. One of her mottoes was, "I see and am silent;" another was, "Always the same."

At one time she devoted herself to the works of the early Christian writers, but she found leisure to complain of the poor portraits that people were making of her. They were not nearly so handsome as she thought they ought to be, and she actually had a proclamation drawn up forbidding all persons to attempt her picture until "some special cunning painter" should produce a satisfactory likeness. Her "loving subjects" were then to be permitted to "follow the said pattern."

For even the most "cunning artist" to satisfy both her Majesty and himself must have been a difficult matter, for she positively forbade having any shade given to her features. "By nature there is no shade in a face," said the queen, "it is only an accident."

Another of her foibles was that of wearing the dress of different countries on different days, one day Italian, the next day French, and so on. It seems not to have been easy to have these gowns made in England, and Elizabeth sent to the continent for a dressmaker. The secretary of state had been the one ordered to draw up the proclamation restraining all save the "cunning artist" yet to be discovered from making her picture, and now we find him ordering the English ambassador to France to "cause" his wife to find the queen "a tailor that hath skill to make her apparel both after the French and the Italian manner." This command was given only a few days after the murder of Lord Darnley which aroused all England.

Elizabeth always enjoyed going about among her subjects, and one of her early visits was to the University of Cambridge. She entered the town on horseback in a habit of black velvet. Her hat was heaped up with feathers, and under it she wore a sort of net, or head-dress, that was all ablaze with precious stones. The beadles of the university gave her their staffs, signifying that all power was in her hands. She could not hold them all, and she gave them back, saying jestingly, "See that you minister justice uprightly, or I will take them into mine hands again." According to ancient custom at a royal visit, she was presented with two pairs of gloves, two sugarloaves, and some confectionery. Long orations were made to her. She was praised as showing forth all the virtues, and although she sometimes interrupted the orators by saying, "That is not true," she commended them at the end so warmly that they had no fear of having offended her.

She did not hesitate to break in upon any speaker, and the next day, when the minister was preaching, she sent a noble lord to tell him to put his cap on. Another high official was despatched to him before he left the pulpit to inform him that the queen liked his sermon. This was on Sunday morning. That evening the chapel was made into a theatre, and an old Latin play was acted for her amusement.

Elizabeth went from college to college, and at each she listened to an oration in her praise and received the usual gift of gloves, sugarloaves, and confectionery. Cambridge had long expected the honor of this visit, and the members of the various learned societies had made preparations for it by composing poems of welcome and praise in Greek, Hebrew, and several other languages. Copies of these verses had been richly bound, and the volume was presented to her as a memorial of her welcome.

All the sermons and speeches and plays were in Latin, and near the close of the queen's stay, a humble petition was made to her that she would speak to her hosts in that language.

"I am but a poor scholar," said she, "but if I might speak my mind in English, I would not stick at the matter."

Then answered the chancellor of the university:—

"Your Highness, in the university nothing English may be said in public."

"Then speak you for me," bade the queen. "The chancellor is the queen's mouth."

"True, your Majesty," he responded, "but I am merely the chancellor of the university; I have not the honor to be the chancellor of your Grace."

After a little more urging, the queen delivered an excellent Latin speech, which she had evidently composed beforehand, and gave the authorities to understand that she should make the university a generous gift either during her life or at her death. This manner of arousing the expectations of her subjects was one of her ways of securing their faithfulness. She used to keep long lists of men of ability and worth, and a man, knowing that his name was on that list, would not fail to be true to her, expecting every day a pension or some other reward of his devotion.

Robert Dudley was high steward of Cambridge, and Elizabeth seems to have exhausted her generous intentions toward the university by presenting him with Kenilworth Castle and manor and other lands. Then it was that she made him Lord Leicester, and when in the ceremony he was kneeling gravely before her with bowed head, this queen of magnificence and barbarism, of subtlety of intellect and coarseness of manner, thought it a brilliant jest to stretch out the royal forefinger to tickle the back of his neck and arouse him from his unwonted seriousness.

CHAPTER IX

ELIZABETH AND PHILIP

HOWEVER fond Elizabeth was of Leicester, she would never allow him to presume upon her favor. A friend of his one day demanded to see the queen, and the usher, or "gentleman of the black rod," as he was called, refused to permit him to enter. Leicester threatened the usher with the loss of his position, but that gentleman went straightway to the queen, fell at her feet, and told the whole story.

"Your Grace," said he, "I have but obeyed your commands, and all that I crave is to know the pleasure of your Majesty. Shall I obey yourself or my Lord Leicester?"

Leicester had also attempted to tell his side of the story, but a wave of the queen's hand had silenced him. Now she turned upon him haughtily and said:—

"I have wished you well, my lord, but know you that my favor is not so locked up in you that others can have no share. I will have here but one mistress and no master."

Leicester tried to take revenge on the queen's vanity by asking her for an appointment in France.

"Do you really wish to go?" she demanded.

"It is one of the things that I most desire," answered the earl. Elizabeth pondered a moment, she glanced at Leicester, and then turned to the Spanish ambassador, who stood near, and said laughingly:—

"I can't live without seeing him. Why, he is my lap-dog, and wherever I go, people expect that he will follow." Leicester did not go to France.

"Elizabeth's old suitor, King Philip, was giving her more trouble than Leicester. The Low Countries, as Holland and Belgium were then called, formed part of his domain. Most of the inhabitants of these lands were Protestants, and they were making a determined resistance to the rule of the Spanish king. Elizabeth believed that if Philip was successful he might attack England. The course decided upon by the English council was to send money secretly to the revolters in the Low Countries. This would not make open war with Spain, but would enable the king's opponents to oppose him more strongly, and would keep him too busy to think of invading England.

Even before Elizabeth came to the throne, the English Channel and the neighboring seas were swarming with bold sailors who attacked any vessel that they believed might be carrying gold or any other cargo of value. To-day this would be called piracy, it was then looked upon as brave seamanship. These pirates cared little for the nationality of a vessel, but Spain had more ships at sea than any other country, and these ships were loaded with gold from America or with valuable goods from India, therefore, Spain was the greatest sufferer; and as the English sailors were generally more bold and more successful than others in making these attacks, the wrath of Spain toward England grew more and more bitter. Whenever a Spanish ship captured an English ship, the sailors were hanged, or imprisoned, or perhaps tortured, or even burned at the stake as heretics. "It is only fair," said Elizabeth, "to get our reprisal in whatever way we can;" and whoever had taken a Spanish vessel, be he English or belonging to some other nation, was allowed to bring his prize into an English port and there dispose of it.

The slave-trade, too, was looked upon as an honorable business and a valuable source of wealth for England. Spain forbade all nations to trade with her American colonies, but these bold Englishmen kidnapped negroes on the African coast, carried them to America, and found ready purchasers in the Spanish colonists of the West Indies. One of these English fleets was attacked by the Spanish in the Gulf of Mexico, and three of the vessels were captured. Elizabeth raged and declared that she would have vengeance. It is possible that her indignation was no less from the fact that two of the vessels of this fleet belonged to the queen herself.

It was not long before the opportunity for revenge appeared. Four Spanish vessels loaded with money for the payment of Philip's army were chased by French pirates and took refuge in an English harbor. Under the pretence of securing the safety of this money, it was quietly transferred to the royal treasury.

The Spanish ambassador protested, but there was much delay before he was permitted to see the queen. He presented a letter from Duke Alva, who commanded the Spanish forces in the Low Countries, claiming the treasure.

"I am not wholly without reason," declared Elizabeth coolly, "for believing that this gold does not belong to the king of Spain."

"This is the duke's own writing, your Highness," said the ambassador.

"Not willingly or with intent to deal unjustly would I seize upon aught that with propriety belongs to his Majesty," said the queen, "but certain rumors have reached me that divers persons of Genoa are sending this money to the Low Countries to make profit by loaning it to the duke."

"Your Majesty, I give you most solemn assurance that such is not the case," declared the helpless ambassador.

"A few days will determine whether your informants or mine be correct," said the queen haughtily. "If the king of Spain can prove that the gold is his, I will restore it to him. Otherwise, I will pay the usual rate of interest to its true owners, and keep it for good service in my own kingdom."

Elizabeth was right in her belief that Philip would not wish to have another war on his hands, and so would make no attack upon her kingdom. He seized Englishmen and English property in Antwerp, but this was small loss to England, for Elizabeth retaliated by imprisoning the Spaniards who were doing business in her kingdom and whose possessions were of far more value than those of the English in Antwerp.

Duke Alva was annoyed and delayed in his plans by the loss of the money, but the fighting went on most bitterly. In France there was a kind of peace between the court and the Huguenots, as the French Protestants were called, but on neither side was there forgiveness or forgetfulness. The leader of the Huguenots was wounded in Paris by an assassin. Catherine de Medicis, mother of the French king, alarmed her son by declaring that the Huguenots would take a fearful vengeance for this attack, and induced him to consent to a terrible slaughter in which thousands of Protestants were slain. This was the massacre of St. Bartholomew's Day.

The English were then thoroughly aroused. Thousands were ready to take up arms and avenge the wicked murders. To the French ambassador fell the unwelcome task of telling the dreadful story to the queen of England. He asked for an audience, but she refused it. For three days she hesitated; at length he was admitted. The queen and all her attendants were dressed in the deepest mourning. The unhappy ambassador entered the room and advanced through the lines of lords and ladies. Little return was made to his respectful salutations, there was dead silence. Finally the queen with grave, stern face, came a few steps toward him, greeted him with politeness, and motioned him to follow her to one side.

"I have no wish to show discourtesy to your sovereign," she said, "but it was impossible that I should bring my mind sooner to speak of a matter so grievous to me and to my realm." The ambassador bowed silently, and the queen went on. "Can it be that this strange news of the prince whom I have so loved and honored has been correctly reported to me?"

"In truth," answered the ambassador gravely, "it is for this very thing that I am come to lament with your Majesty over the sad accident."

"An accident?" questioned Elizabeth.

"Surely, your Majesty, for is not that an accident which is forced upon a sovereign by no will of his own, but by the plots and treasons of those whom he would gladly have befriended?"

"How may that be?" asked Elizabeth.

"The evening before the sad event the king was horrified to learn that in revenge for the attempt at assassination, a terrible deed had been planned. It was no less than the imprisonment of himself and his family and the murder of the Catholic leaders."

"How was this known?"

"One whose conscience could no longer bear the burden revealed the wicked plot. The words and looks of several of the conspirators gave gloomy confirmation to the story."

"Why not imprison the traitors? Is there no dungeon in France and no executioner?"

"Your Majesty, not all rulers have your keen judgment and your control of even the strongest sentiments of your heart. The king has not yet learned to govern his feelings by moderation. He had but a few short hours to decide what was best. Many were urging him on to inflict the most severe penalties, and at last he yielded, and allowed that to be done which he will ever regret. Especially does he lament that with a populace so wildly excited and so indignant at the plot against the king, it is all but impossible that some who are innocent should not have perished with the guilty. This is his chief cause of grief." The ambassador had made as smooth a story as possible, but how would the queen receive it?

She was silent for several minutes, then she said:—

"Although I could not accept his Majesty, the king of France, for a husband, yet shall I always revere him as if I were his wife, and ever feel jealous for his honor. I will believe that from some strange accident, which time will perhaps more fully explain, these murders have come to pass. I recommend the Protestants among his people as especially entitled to his Highness's loving care and protection."

When this speech was reported to Catherine de Medicis, she smiled grimly and said, "The queen of England can hardly ask greater protection than she herself grants; namely, to force no man's conscience, but to permit no other worship in the land than that which the ruler himself practises."

Four years had passed since Mary of Scotland fled to England. Nothing had been satisfactorily determined in regard to her guilt or innocence. An important part of the testimony against her was a casket of her letters to Bothwell. Elizabeth's commissioners believed these letters to be the work of Mary's hand, but the English queen refused to permit them to be made public. Whether they were true or were forgeries, she would not allow a queen, a member of her own family, to be declared guilty of murder.

Mary was put under the care of the Earl of Shrewsbury. The sovereign claimed the right to give prisoners of state or guests of the nation to her nobles for watch or entertainment or both. "I am about to trust you as I would trust few men," the queen said to the earl when she informed him of his new task. He was obliged to accept the charge meekly, but it must have been a heavy burden. If his family moved from one of his manors to another, Mary must go with them. She must have the attendance and treatment due to her rank, but she must be closely watched to prevent, if possible, the sending of letters and messages to any that might conspire to rescue her. Guests of the family must be kept from meeting her. It is no wonder that the earl's health gave out. He went away for medical treatment, and at once there came a letter from Cecil:—

"The queen has heard that you are gone from home. She says she can scarce believe it, but she bids me know from you what order you left for attendance upon the Queen of Scots. She would not that you should be long away from her, for she feels it only in

119

accordance with her honor that the said queen be honorably attended, and for this she cares as much as for any question of surety."

The earl did not recover at once, and the queen sent another trusty servant to take charge of Mary. The caring for the prisoner and her retinue was no small matter, for there were so many in her train that her unwilling host felt greatly relieved when Elizabeth commanded that their number be reduced to thirty.

Soon after Mary's coming to England there was an uprising in the north among the nobles who wished to oblige Elizabeth to acknowledge Mary as her heir. They planned for the Scotch queen to marry an English duke of great power and wealth. This conspiracy was discovered, Mary was kept for a while in closer confinement, and after some time the duke was beheaded. Elizabeth long refused to sign the warrant, and she would pay no attention whatever to the counsels of the royal advisers in regard to the execution of Mary, though one called her "that dangerous woman," another, "a desperate person." The archbishop of York advised Elizabeth to "cut off the Scottish queen's head forthwith;" Cecil was decidedly in favor of this plan, for he believed that it was the only way to secure peace to the kingdom, that so long as Mary lived there would be plots, and that, however closely she was watched, she would find means to communicate with plotters. The rebellion in the north was the only revolt of any importance while Elizabeth was on the throne. It was punished most severely by a vast number of executions.

Not long after the revolt, the Pope excommunicated Elizabeth. He pronounced upon her a solemn curse whether she ate or drank, went in or went out; whatever she did, she was accursed, and her subjects were no longer called upon to obey her. Neither Philip nor the king of France ventured to have this decree published in his kingdom, and in England it seems to have produced no effect whatever. The government was every day becoming stronger. The man who disobeyed did not often escape punishment, and Englishmen in general preferred to be excommunicated by the Pope in Italy than to be executed by Elizabeth in England.

The queen gained steadily in power and in the affections of her subjects. Some of this increase of power was because by good management England had grown richer, some of it because by her shrewd treatment of France and Spain she had won the deference of both. Her means of gaining power were not always to be commended; she was not above maintaining nominally peaceful relations with a king while she was aiding his revolting subjects; and she would favor first one proposed marriage and then another, as it might suit her purposes to win the good will of the country to which the respective wooers belonged. When she was once accused of deriding and mocking whoever sought her hand, she replied with an air of injured innocence that she never "mocked or trifled" with any of those who would have had her in marriage, that she had given them her answer as promptly as the "troubles and hindrances that were happening in the world" would permit. Dishonorable as her behavior sometimes was, it is only fair to Elizabeth to remember that in her times fair dealing among nations was the exception rather than the rule; the country that could gain the advantage over another country was looked upon as having shown the greater ability.

Part of Elizabeth's gain in power was due to the improved condition of England. The country was at peace, taxes were not large; ways of living were becoming more comfortable; all subjects were required to attend the Protestant church, but fines and loss of office were small matters when compared with the axe and the stake; bold sailors were taking English ships to distant harbors; a great exchange had been built in London where merchants from any part of the world might come to buy and sell; and the thing that made all these advantages possible was the fact that the government was firm and sure. That the queen was the vainest woman who ever lived, that she would say one thing one day and quite another thing the next morning was perhaps not known outside of her court, and in any case, her subjects would have forgiven her faults, for they felt that she was ever a friend to them, that she believed in them and trusted them. At one time a gun went off by accident and the bullet came very near the queen. Elizabeth straightway issued a proclamation, "I will believe nothing against my subjects," said she, "that loving parents would not believe of their children."

Elizabeth refused positively to stand at the head of any one party; she was determined to be, as she said, "a good queen" to all her subjects. It must be admitted that she was sometimes unjust to the "great folk," but nothing else aroused her wrath so surely and so dangerously as a wrong done to her people, to the masses of her subjects, with whom she felt sympathy and to whom she turned for support. It was an ancient custom in the land that whenever the sovereign went from one part of the kingdom to another, the people of whatever district he might chance to be in should furnish him with food for his attendants, often numbered by hundreds. "Purveyors," or officers whose business it was to attend to the providing of food, went ahead of the royal party and took what they chose to declare would be needed. Sometimes they paid for it—whatever price they chose—sometimes they did not, but in any case the purveyor was sorely tempted to seize larger quantities of supplies than would be needed and sell them elsewhere. When Elizabeth discovered that one of her officers had been behaving in this manner, she was most indignant. "My people shall suffer by no such abuses," she declared. One article that the cheating purveyor had seized and sold for the advantage of his own pocket was a quantity of smelts. "Take him to the pillory," bade the angry queen. "Hang the smelts about his neck, and see you to it that there shall he sit for three full days. Let him who steals from my people keep in his account that he has to reckon not with them but with me; they are *my* people, and I am their queen."

This proud sovereign who ruled her haughty nobles with so high a hand enjoyed showing to her subjects how humble she could be. When she was tormenting the king of Spain by every means in her power, she kept on one Maundy Thursday the old custom of feet-washing. Elizabeth was thirty-nine years of age, and therefore the poor women who were seated before her for the ceremony were thirty-nine in number. The queen's ladies brought silver basins filled with warm water delicately perfumed with flowers and sweet-smelling herbs. Cushions were placed, and on these the queen kneeled as she washed one foot of each of the poor women, marked it with a cross and kissed it. It takes a little from the humility of the act to read that just before the queen's performance of this duty the feet of the thirty-nine poor women were most carefully scrubbed and perfumed by three separate officials. There must have been some competition to be among the chosen thirty-nine, if any one guessed what would happen, for before the queen bade them farewell, she presented each one with a pair of shoes, cloth for a gown, the towel and apron used in the ceremony, a purse of white leather containing thirty-nine pence, and a red purse containing twenty shillings. Besides these gifts, each one received bread, fish, and wine.

It is no wonder that Elizabeth was popular among her subjects, and that she rejoiced in their good will, but some of the consequences of their devotion were not agreeable. It was the custom to wear ornaments called aglets, which were somewhat like large loops. These were made of gold and often set with precious stones. They were sewed upon various parts of her robes of state, and they had a fashion of disappearing when the queen was dining in public, for her subjects who were near enough to secure one as a souvenir of their beloved queen seem to have taken advantage of their opportunity. The persons who had charge of her wardrobe made in their books many such entries as these:—

"Lost from her Majesty's back the 17th of January, at Westminster, one aglet of gold, enamelled blue, set upon a gown of purple velvet."

Another one is:—

"One pearl and a tassel of gold being lost from her Majesty's back, off the French gown of black satin, the 15th day of July, at Greenwich."

CHAPTER X

ENTERTAINING A QUEEN

MANY a monarch has liked to wander about his domains in disguise and hear what his subjects had to say about him when they did not suspect that he was near. Elizabeth thoroughly enjoyed journeying about her kingdom, but she did not wish to be disguised, she preferred that everyone should know where she was and should be able to sing her praises in such wise that she need not lose the pleasure of hearing them. These journeys of hers were called progresses, and while on a progress she was always entertained by some wealthy subject.

Whenever there was a rumor that the queen meant to leave town, every nobleman who owned a beautiful country seat would tremble, for while a royal visit was an honor, it was also a vast expense and responsibility. The queen would set out with a great retinue, but for what place no one was told until a few days before the journey began. If there was the least reason to think that she would go to a certain district, the noblemen of that district hastened to engage provisions of all sorts. The luckless favorite was at last told that the great honor of entertaining his sovereign was to be bestowed upon him. He had to appear exceedingly grateful and to make humble speeches of thankfulness, even though he was wondering between the words where he could buy meat and fish and fruit and other food for a great company.

As soon as the queen's messengers were out of sight, then was there a hurrying and a scurrying. In one case many of the nobles in a certain district were so afraid of being victims that they engaged all the provisions in the vicinity, and the unfortunate man who was first chosen had to send post-haste to Flanders to buy food for his unwelcome guests. One man provided for a royal visit of three days wheat, rye, oats, butter, partridges, trout, lobsters, beer, ale, wine, sugar loaves, turkeys, pheasants, salmon, deer, sheep, oysters, plums, preserved lemons, sweetmeats, cinnamon water, beef, ling, sturgeons, pigeons, etc. These eatables had to be obtained in large quantities; for instance, this three-days' host bought fifty-two dozen chickens for one item, and twenty bushels of salt for another.

Nor was this all. Damask, knives, and pewter dishes must be hired; carpenters and bricklayers must be engaged to make all sorts of changes in the house and grounds that might suit the whim of a queen who did not hesitate to express her opinions if she was displeased. Moreover, when this queen was entertained, she expected to find entertainment; dancers must be hired, and perhaps a whole company of actors must be engaged to present a play for her pleasure.

It is not at all wonderful that even the richest of Elizabeth's subjects dreaded a visit from their queen.

The archbishop of Canterbury wrote a most pitiful letter about the difficulty of finding bedrooms for so great a party. He explained what he had planned, and ended, "Here is as much as I am able to do in this house." One man who had been notified that the queen would soon honor his castle wrote to Cecil, "I trust you will provide that her Majesty's stay be not above two nights and a day," and he added anxiously, "I pray God that the room and lodgings may be to her content."

This man, like the rest of Elizabeth's hosts, was not anxious without good reason, for the queen often manifested but slight gratitude for the efforts of her entertainers, while she seldom hesitated to express her disapproval if anything occurred that did not please her. At one house she discovered by chance an image of the Virgin Mary, and within a fortnight her host was in prison on the charge of being a Catholic. To another house she made an unexpected visit when the owner was away from home. The unfortunate lord had a fine deer park in which he took great pride, but on his return he found that large numbers of the deer had been slaughtered to amuse the queen and her retinue. He was so indignant that he "disparked" the ground. It seems that it was not safe for a man to do what he would with his own, for not many weeks later a friend of his at court wrote to him:—

"Her Majesty has been informed that you were not pleased at the good sport she had in your park. Have a wary watch over your words and deeds. It was Leicester who brought her to your castle. He has taken no small liking to it, and it might easily be that he would claim to have good title to the same."

The most brilliant of Elizabeth's entertainments was given her by Robert Dudley at Kenilworth Castle not long after he became Lord Leicester. For nineteen days he was her host, but he could well afford to make the outlay, for the queen's recent gifts to him were valued at £50,000, an amount that was worth as much then as a million and a quarter dollars to-day.

On this visit Elizabeth was received at a neighboring town and was feasted in a great tent. Then after a day's hunting she and her train arrived at the fine old castle with its manor lands of hill and dale, forest and pasture. It was already eight in the evening, but there were all sorts of sights for her to see before she entered the castle. First came forth ten sibyls in white silk, gleaming in the soft twilight. One of them made a speech of welcome, and the company passed into the tilt-yard. There stood a tall porter, big of limb and stern of countenance. He brandished a heavy club as he strutted to and fro, apparently talking to himself. He did not know, he declared, what all this chattering, riding, and trudging up and down was for, but he did not like it, and there was no one great enough to deserve it. Suddenly he saw the queen, and was so overcome by her beauty—so he said in his speech—that he could only fall down on his knees before her and beg her pardon. He gave her his keys and called his six trumpeters to announce the arrival of so wondrous a being.

On two sides of the castle there was a beautiful pool, and as the queen stepped upon the bridge that crossed an arm of the mere, a sudden light gleamed far out on the lake, and over the quiet water came a little floating island, all ablaze with torches. On the island was the fair Lady of the Lake, and with her were two attendant nymphs. The Lady recited a pretty poem to the purport that ever since King Arthur's days she had been hidden, not daring to come forth, but now a royal guest had come for whom she could feel as deep a love as for Arthur himself. She ended:—

"Pass on, madame, you need no longer stand,
The lake, the lodge, the lord are yours for to command."

With all her quickness of wit, Elizabeth could think of no better reply than, "We had thought the lake had been ours; and do you call it yours now? Well, we will herein commune more with you hereafter." Then came a great flourish of shawms, cornets, and other musical instruments, and the queen passed on. She was as eager as a child to see what was to be the next sight, for nothing gave her more pleasure than these displays.

Everyone was interested in mythology in those days, and no entertainment was regarded as complete without some reference to the gods and goddesses; cooks often represented in their pastry scenes from the stories of the early deities. Elizabeth's way now led over a bridge that crossed the lower court and extended to the entrance of the castle. On either hand were seven pairs of wooden pillars, each pair loaded

130

with the gift of some god. On the first pair were the tokens of Sylvanus, god of the woodfowl; these were great cages containing various kinds of birds, alive and fluttering in the glare of the torches. Then came Pomona's treasures, two large silver bowls full of the fairest apples, pears, cherries and nuts. White and red grapes represented the welcome of Bacchus, while on the fifth pair of pillars were the gifts of Neptune, herring, oysters, and mullets, for the god of the sea as well as the deities of the woods and the fields had been summoned to give greeting to Elizabeth. Mars was not forgotten; well polished bows and arrows, gleaming swords and spears shone in the flaring lights. The last pillars bore the offering of Apollo, the cornet, flute, and harp, the lute, viol, and shawm.

At the end of this bridge was an arch whereon was written a lengthy welcome in Latin. The letters were white, but wherever the queen's name appeared, it shone out in yellow gold. Leicester had no idea of trusting the flickering light of torches to reveal all these elaborate preparations for the queen's reception, and beside the arch stood a poet with a wreath of bays on his head. His part was to explain to her what each offering signified and to read the inscription over the gateway. It is to be hoped that the lights shone upon him well and clearly, for he was attired in all the splendor of a long robe of blue silk with sleeves flowing widely to reveal glimpses of his gorgeous crimson doublet.

As the queen alighted from her horse and entered the castle, every clock in the building was stopped, perhaps to suggest that she would never grow old, that even time had no power over her. She was escorted to her rooms, and then came the welcome of Jupiter, king of the gods. This was peal after peal of the guns of the castle and a display of fireworks. For two long hours this greeting of Jupiter's blazed and roared, but it was none too long to please the woman for whom it had been planned.

The next day was Sunday, and the queen went to church, but in the afternoon came music and dancing, and at night more fireworks, stars and streams and hail of fire and burning darts flashing through the darkness. This was only the beginning of the festivities. The next afternoon there was a hunt, and many a deer was slain to amuse the royal guest. A "savage man," covered with moss and ivy, came out of the forest as she was riding back to the castle and made her a long speech, declaring that never before had he seen so glorious a sight. He called nymphs and fauns and dryads and satyrs to his aid, but no one could tell the meaning of the vision. At last he held a conversation with Echo, and learned how mighty a queen was before him. Then he made another speech about her wondrous beauty, her grace and manner, and the rare qualities of her mind. Finally, to show his submission, he broke his stick into pieces. Unfortunately, this action startled the queen's horse. There was confusion for a moment, and all flocked around in utter dismay lest some harm had befallen her. "No hurt, no hurt," said Elizabeth graciously, and the officer who wrote the account of the visit says, "These words were the best part of the play."

There was a mock fight; some Italians gave an exhibition of "leaps, springs, and windings," and so agile were they that the chronicler says it could hardly be distinguished whether they were "man or spirit." There was a bridal procession of a rustic couple who were delighted to have the opportunity to appear before the queen. The groom was "lame of a leg broken in his youth at football," but he made up for the loss by wearing a mighty pair of harvest gloves to show that he was a good husbandman, while on his back was slung a pen and inkhorn to indicate that he was "bookish." On his head was a straw hat with a crown made steeple-shape. He and his bride were escorted by the young folk of the parish, each man wearing a bit of green broom fastened to his left arm, and carrying an alder pole in his right hand by way of spear. One wore a hat, another a cap; one rejoiced in a coat or a jerkin, while another had only doublet and hose; one had boots without spurs, and another had spurs without boots, while a third had neither; but it was a merry time, for were they not all come to display themselves before the glorious queen?

So the days went on. There was another scene on the lake when a dolphin, eighty feet long, came swimming up to meet Elizabeth. On his back was the god Arion, who had come from regions far away that he might sing to her, and within the machine were six players with their instruments. There was a show of bear-baiting, wherein thirteen bears tied to stakes, were attacked by a company of dogs trained for the purpose. To see them clawing and tumbling and growling and scratching and biting, to note the bears' watchfulness for their enemies and the dogs' keenness in getting the better of the bears, was what the letter-writing official called "a very pleasant sport." This seems to have been the general opinion of the cruel amusement, for a bear-baiting was often arranged as a treat for the entertainment of foreign ambassadors and other national guests of rank and dignity.

The day's pastime was often closed by thundering peals of guns and by fireworks that would "mount in the air and burn in the water." Often the whole castle was illuminated by candle, fire, and torchlight, as if the god of the sun himself—so said one who was there—was resting in its chambers instead of taking his nightly course to the antipodes. There was surely no lack of amusements, and indeed several spectacles had been planned for which there was no time. One man who was to represent a minstrel of the olden days was sorely grieved because he could not have the honor of singing before the queen. He found what comfort he might, however, in showing his skill to a company of the courtiers. One of them described his appearance, and a reader cannot help feeling sorry that Queen Elizabeth lost the sight. The "ancient minstrel" wore a long, flowing robe of green, gathered at the throat and fastened with a clasp. The wide sleeves were slit from shoulder to hand, and under them was a closely fitting undersleeve of white cotton. He wore a black worsted doublet, confined at the waist by a wide red girdle. His shoes were "not new indeed, but shining," though perhaps not quite so brilliantly as was his hair, for that had been smoothed with a sponge "dipped in a little bear's grease" till it gleamed like a duck's wing. He wore a shirt whose bosom was ruffled, and starched "after the new trink," till every ruffle stood up stiff and "glittering." A handkerchief was thrust into his bosom, but enough of it was displayed to show that it was edged with bright blue lace and marked with a heart. Around his neck was a broad red ribbon which held his harp, while on a green lacing hung the tuning key. It was really a pity that the queen lost all this display.

The chief reason for Elizabeth's pleasure in these progresses was probably her delight in all pageants and thorough enjoyment of her popularity among the people. At such times she was nearer to them than at any others. The humblest servant in the castle where she was making her stay, the simplest peasant of the countryside, had as free access to her Majesty as the greatest of her nobles. Anyone might bring her a petition, anyone might offer her a gift; and no matter of how slight value the present might be, its donor was never disappointed in the gracious thanks that he hoped to receive from his sovereign. Often sufferers from scrofula were brought before her with the prayer that she would but lay her hand upon them, for England had believed for six hundred years that the touch of the royal hand would cure this disease. It was said that on Elizabeth's visit to Kenilworth she healed nine.

This was only one of the many superstitions of the Elizabethan times. A bit of the wood of which the gallows was made would cure the ague; wearing a topaz stone would bring an insane man to his right mind; a verse of the Bible written on parchment and worn about the neck would drive away evil spirits; to carry fern-seed in the pocket would enable a man to "go invisible." Powdered diamonds would heal one disease; wiping the face with a red cloth another; while pills made of the powdered skull of a man that had been hanged were a sure remedy for a third. Not only the ignorant but most of the most learned men of the day believed firmly in astrology, and the home of the queen's astrologer, Dr. Dee, was often crowded with nobles who were eager to know the fates foretold to them by the heavens. There was so firm a belief in witchcraft that one of the queen's bishops preached before her on the subject, telling her what sufferings her subjects were enduring from witches. "They pine away even unto the death," said he, and he begged her Majesty to make a law providing for the punishment of sorcerers. This was done, or rather, an old law was revived. When Elizabeth had a toothache, many of her advisers declared that the pain had been produced by magic, and it was suggested that the treatment of waxen images of the queen at the hands of some who were ill-disposed toward her was the reason for her sufferings. The royal physicians could not agree upon the cause of the trouble or upon a remedy, and the matter was ended by the council of state taking charge of the affair and ordering a prescription from a foreign physician.

At the time of Queen Elizabeth's progress to Kenilworth, a banquet was arranged for her. One of her courtiers says that it was neither well served nor nicely set down, that it was "disorderly wasted and coarsely consumed," that it was carried on "more curtly than courteously;" but he adds, "If it might

Kenilworth in Elizabeth's time.—*From an old print.*

please and be liked and do that it came for, then was all well enough."

The Elizabethan life was a strange mingling of magnificence and discomfort. There were most palatial mansions with noble towers and gateways and terraces, with lawns and gardens and fountains and parks and wide-spreading acres of hill and dale, of field and forest, but according to modern ideas there was little comfort in all this splendor. The only way to warm these lordly castles was by an occasional fireplace, and the rooms were full of drafts that even the heavy tapestry hung on the walls would not prevent. Cleanliness was almost unknown. Floors were strewn with rushes, and when a room was to be put in order, fresh rushes were brought in, but no one thought it at all necessary to carry away the old ones. A room was almost never swept unless space was needed for dancing; then a circle in the middle was cleared of rushes, dirt, dust, crumbs and bones from the dining table and all sorts of rubbish that had accumulated since the time of the last merrymaking. One letter-writer of the day declared that the rushes on floors not needed for dancing were sometimes left for twenty years without being swept away. Whoever could afford it owned several country houses, and when one became absolutely unendurable, even according to sixteenth century notions, he would move to another to let the first house "sweeten," as was said.

The list of different kinds of food purchased for the queen's progress gives an idea of what the rich folk ate, that is, what they ate in the summer. In the winter they had little besides salt meat, various kinds of bread, and the most remarkable pies that one ever heard of. They were made of everything from artichokes to herring. One pastry is described as made of fish and flavored with pepper, ginger, and cloves. The artichoke pies were made of a combination of artichokes, marrow, ginger, raisins and dates. Few vegetables were used. Potatoes had been brought from America, but they were regarded as a luxury. They were roasted in the embers or else boiled and eaten with pepper, oil, and vinegar. There was neither tea nor coffee; beer or wine was drunk at every meal. People ate with knives and fingers, for forks did not appear until near the end of Elizabeth's life. One that was richly jeweled was presented to her and was kept in a glass case as a curiosity.

The homes of the poor were indeed bare and comfortless. The floors were of clay or beaten earth. A clumsy table, some wooden stools, a wooden trencher to hold the food, a pile of straw to sleep on, salt fish and rye or barley bread—these were all the comforts that a poor man could expect to have in his home. The house itself was built of boughs of trees interwoven with willow twigs and daubed with clay. The fire was made against a rock set into one of the walls, and the smoke found its way out as best it could. Before the reign of Elizabeth was over, chimneys had become more common, and many men whose fathers had lived in huts of mud and had eaten from wooden trenchers were building for themselves houses of oak with the comfort of a chimney and perhaps the elegance of a pewter porringer or two among their wooden dishes. At best the luxuries were not very luxurious, but a writer of the time lamented that men were no longer as brave and strong as they used to be, and thought their weakness was due to these dainty, and enfeebling fashions.

CHAPTER XI

ELIZABETH'S SUITORS

NEVER before did the hand of a woman and its possible bestowal in marriage play so important a part in the affairs of Europe as did that of Elizabeth. She contrived to delay and postpone giving an answer to Philip till his minister wrote home wrathfully, "The English queen is possessed of ten thousand devils," but at the death of Philip's third wife, ten years later, she was not at all displeased when the Spanish ambassador suggested pointedly that Philip was "still young enough to take a fourth wife." When France was showing too much favor to Scotland to suit English notions, she was fully capable of discussing the possibility of a Scotch husband, and when there was a whisper that one foreign ruler meditated the rescue of the captive Mary and a marriage with her, Elizabeth at once sent an agent to him to suggest a marriage with herself. Whenever her fears of Spain increased, she began to think of a French alliance. There was always a French suitor ready, for Catherine de Medicis was trying her best to persuade Elizabeth to choose one of the French princes for a husband.

The English queen kept one suitor waiting in uncertainty for seven years, another for eleven. She had all sorts of absurd names for her admirers; one was her "lap-dog," one her "tame cat," one her "sheep," another her "frog." Occasionally she found a wooer who was not so ready as the others to await her royal pleasure. Three years after all negotiations with the Archduke Charles, brother of the German emperor, had been broken off, she was talking familiarly with some of the ladies of the bedchamber, and she said with some indignation:—

"The king of France is to marry one daughter of the emperor, and the king of Spain is to marry another."

"There's many a noble marriage, your Majesty," said one of her ladies. "Would that there was one more," she added slily.

"These royal brides have near of kin to promote their interests," replied Elizabeth. "What can a woman alone do for herself, whether she is on a throne or on a wooden stool?"

"Your Grace has full many a faithful servant," answered the lady, "who would be ready to give life and limb to do your will."

"And yet with all these honorable marriages a-making, not one man in the council had the wit to remind the rest that the emperor has a brother," said the queen and turned away abruptly. The lady understood what was expected of her, and she sent at once for the Earl of Leicester.

"Would you do aught to gratify her Majesty?" she asked.

"Is there aught that I would not do to gratify her Majesty—or yourself?" he added with a gallant bow. The lady repeated the conversation.

The next day a humble petition came from the council:—

"Far be it from the intentions of your Majesty's servants to suggest anything displeasing to your Grace, but if it be in accordance with your will, it would be highly gratifying to your councilors, should you grant this their humble petition that your Highness will consider the matter of the Archduke Charles and the suit that he so recently made."

Elizabeth replied:—

"Of my own will the thought of marriage has ever been far from me, but I cannot refuse the request of my councilors in whose judgment I have so much confidence."

An ambassador was sent at once to the German emperor with the message:—

"The queen of England regrets deeply that her frequent illnesses, the wars in France and Flanders, and difficult matters in her own government have prevented her from returning a final answer to the suit of his imperial Majesty's brother. If he is pleased to come to England, he will be most welcome, and she doubts not that her subjects can be persuaded to permit him the free exercise of his own religion."

"It is a pleasure," returned the emperor, "to send to her Majesty, the queen of England, assurances of my warmest regard. Most highly do I esteem the honor of receiving a message from a sovereign of such beauty of face and greatness of mind;" and then he continued, not without a little enjoyment it may be, "My brother is most grateful for her Majesty's good intentions toward him, but he would say that after a delay of three years he had supposed that she did not wish to accept his suit, and he is now engaged to a princess of his own faith, but he earnestly hopes that the queen will ever regard him as a brother."

The youthful envoy was presented with a silver vessel and treated with all courtesy, but these attentions to her ambassador did not soothe the rage of Elizabeth. "If I were a man," she stormed, "and the emperor had offered me such an insult, I would have called him out to single combat."

The last of Elizabeth's wooers was the Duke of Alençon. Catherine de Medicis had tried hard to win the hand of the queen for an older son who was not at all eager for the honor. When this plan failed, Catherine wrote to her minister in England: "Would she have my son Alençon? He is turned of sixteen, though but little for his age." She went on to say that this youth had the understanding, visage, and demeanor of one much older than he is." Elizabeth was thirty-eight, and when the scheme was first proposed to Cecil, he exclaimed, "Why, it would look like a mother with her son."

Elizabeth never refused a suitor at once, and she demanded full information about the Duke of Alençon. "How tall is he?" she asked. The duke was really so stunted as to be almost dwarfed; he had an enormous nose, a wide mouth, and a face scarred by the smallpox.

"I have waited a long time," said the queen, "and if I should now marry a man so much younger than myself and so badly marked with the pox, indeed I know not what they would say."

"The duke is growing older every day," replied the French ambassador, "and in London there is a learned physician who declares that in two or three days he can remove all traces of the disease. The duke's heart is full of love and admiration for your Majesty. If I might venture, but no——" and he thrust back into his pocket a paper that he had partly drawn forth.

"What is that?" demanded Elizabeth.

"Pardon, your Majesty, but it is a paper that I have no right to show. This is but the private letter of the duke, and was not meant to fall under the eyes of your Grace." Finally he was prevailed upon to give her the paper, which proved to be a note—written expressly for the purpose—from Alençon to a friend in France. She read and reread.

"That is a fair penmanship," said she. "That is marvelously well done."

"And the matter of the letter," asked the ambassador, "is not that, too, well done? It is but the outpourings of an honest heart and of its longings to win your Grace for himself."

"It is very fairly written," said Elizabeth, and she ended the audience, but she did not return the note.

The duke wrote many letters to the queen, and they do have an air of sincerity and earnestness that is different from the writings of some of Elizabeth's suitors. Catherine sent word that the learned doctor from London was doing much to improve the appearance of her son's face, but she wished to be sure that the medicines were harmless. "He can easily practise on a page," she wrote, "and if it does well, he can use his remedies on my son." The French ambassador hastened to tell the good news to Elizabeth, but this disappointing sovereign replied coolly, "I am really surprised that so loving a mother did not attempt sooner to remove so great a disfigurement."

One June day a young man with two servants appeared at Elizabeth's gates and demanded to see the queen. It was Alençon himself, and she was delighted. Of all her wooers not one before had ever dared to come to England and run the risk of a refusal, but "Monsieur," as the English called him, had shown himself so bold that the queen was charmed. He was homely, there was no denying it, but he was brave and gallant, quick and sprightly, and one of the best flatterers that had ever been at the English court. His reception and entertainment were most cordial, and he went home in full expectation of marrying the queen.

Not long after this visit Elizabeth called her council to consider the marriage. Cecil in his usual methodical fashion drew up a paper with the advantages on the left and the disadvantages on the right. Finally the council reported to the sovereign that they would try to "conform themselves" to whatever she wished. Then the queen was angry, for she had expected them to urge her to marry. She cried and she stormed. She told her councilors that they cared nothing at all for her safety and the welfare of the kingdom. They bore her wrath with the utmost humility, but they did not change their report. Neither did the queen change her mind, and the marriage treaty was drawn up. The councilors did not despair even then, and one evening a well-arranged scene took place after the queen had retired to her chamber. Her ladies fell on their knees around her. They sobbed and groaned.

"Oh, your Majesty," said one, "such a step cannot bring you happiness."

"The duke is so young," lamented another. "He knows not how to conceive of your greatness. He will despise you and scorn you because he cannot appreciate such rare excellence of mind. Only a king should be your husband."

"Your Majesty, do not forget Queen Mary," one wailed. "Think of her misery, and do not bring another foreigner into the land."

"How can a queen be governor of the Protestant church and promise to obey a Catholic spouse?" asked one.

Elizabeth turned sharply away without a word, but in the morning she sent for the duke.

"Your Grace," said he with great concern, "it grieves me to the heart to see you pale and tearful."

"Good reason have I for pallor," said she, "for two more nights like the last would bring me to the grave. The woman who lives in a cottage may wed whom she will; the queen of England must wed to please her subjects."

The duke dashed away to his own apartment. "England may well be an island," he exclaimed, "for the women are as changeable as the waves that encircle it." The queen had given him a ring, and now he threw it into the farthest corner of the room. He would have left England at once, but Elizabeth would not permit him to go, and when after three months he declared that he would stay no longer, she persisted in going to Canterbury with him, much against his will. He left her weeping, and while he was crossing the Channel, she was writing a poem beginning:—

> "I grieve yet dare not show my discontent;
> I love, and yet am forced to seem to hate."

"Monsieur" was the last of Elizabeth's suitors. Eleven years had passed since his marriage with the queen had first been discussed. She was now fifty years of age; the country settled into the belief that she would never marry, and most people expected that the next ruler of England would be the son of Mary, the prisoner.

No one knows whether Elizabeth was in earnest or not in any of the plans for her marriage. Leicester said: "Should she decide to marry, I am all but convinced that she would choose no other than myself,— at least, she has done me the honor to say as much— but I know not what to hope or what to fear." In the early part of her reign her subjects were nearly equally divided into Catholics and Protestants. It was her policy to be a Protestant, but to do nothing that would arouse the Catholics against her, as a Protestant marriage would surely have done. If on the other hand she had chosen a Catholic, then the ruling power of the country would have been enraged. She declared over and over that she would never marry one of her own subjects, and she had not forgotten the indignation of the English when Mary persisted in marrying a foreigner. Two things were worth more to this queen than all else in the world; one was the love of her subjects, the other was her own power. Any marriage that she might make would deprive her in some degree of one or the other. Her word could not always be trusted, but there is certainly some reason for believing that she was truthful in declaring that she did not mean to marry, and that if she changed her mind, it would be only to obey the demand of the country.

At the same time she enjoyed fancying herself in love with one or another. She demanded the utmost adoration from her courtiers. Few men could be comfortable at her court who did not bow down to her as the wisest, wittiest, most brilliant, most beautiful of women. When half of Europe was raving over the beauty of Mary, Queen of Scots, Elizabeth did her best to oblige Mary's ambassador to admit that she herself was far more lovely. She often spoke of herself as the "old woman," but woe to the courtier who did not hasten to assure her that such beauty as hers could never change, that each day only made her more radiant. She was always indignant when any of her courtiers ventured to marry, but perhaps this wrath was not so very illogical, for when they had assured her hundreds of times that all other beauty paled before hers, that nothing in the world save the radiance of her smile could cheer their lives, how could she help being enraged when they proved by marriage that her favor alone would not raise them to the heights of happiness? At last even her favorite Leicester married. Then Elizabeth raged. She sent him to prison, and would have committed him to the Tower, had not one of her most trusted councilors opposed her lawless proceedings so strongly.

The older Elizabeth grew, the more gorgeous became her raiment. When she was living quietly at Hatfield House with Mary wearing the crown, she dressed with exceeding plainness and simplicity. It was her best policy then to attract as little notice as possible; but when she was once safely on the throne, she showed herself a true daughter of Henry VIII. in her love of magnificence. She thoroughly enjoyed riding through streets hung with tapestry; she liked to see flags and streamers fluttering from the windows of the houses; processions, pageants, shows of all kinds were her delight. As she proved at Kenilworth, she could partake of a public banquet, ride on a hunt for half a day, listen to addresses of welcome and explanation of spectacles produced in her honor; and after so well-filled a day she could hear the thunder of guns and watch the flashing of fireworks for two hours longer without the least sign of weariness.

It is true that when she was alone with her ladies, she was satisfied with a comparatively simple dress, but when she was in public and felt herself part of the magnificence, nothing could be too sumptuous. Cloth of silver, cloth of gold, the richest of Italian velvet, the heaviest of silk, these were her robes, and there were fully two thousand of them. Nor were they plain in their richness; some were covered with pictures of eyes and ears to suggest that whatever was said or done in the land would come to the knowledge of the queen. Some were covered with embroidered illustrations of tales from mythology, or various devices that were full of some hidden significance. Aglets of all kinds adorned her gowns, as did buttons and clasps made of gold and enameled or set lavishly with diamonds or pearls or rubies. Her various kinds of head-dresses were marvels, for they were so a-glitter with precious stones. While Mary of Scotland was a captive, she sent Elizabeth a new year's gift of a net-work head-dress which she herself had made. A little later the French ambassador brought the queen three embroidered nightcaps, also made by the fair hands of Mary.

"In faith, I thank the Queen of Scots," said Elizabeth, "but my council be now but scarce recovered from their commotion and jealousy because you brought me a new year's gift from the same lady."

The disappointed ambassador went home with the nightcaps, but at the next call his luck was better.

Elizabeth had determined to accept the pretty present, whether the act pleased her council or not. "Tell the Queen of Scots," said she, "that I am older than she is. When people arrive at my age, they take all they can get with both hands, and only give with their little finger." This was indeed true, for Elizabeth's hand was always open to a gift, especially to one of personal adornment. When her godson would win a favor from her, he presented her with a "heart of gold, garnished with sparks of rubies." Her silk-woman brought her one new year's day a pair of black silk stockings, a rare luxury even for a queen, since Spain was the home of silk stockings, and from the land of Elizabeth's rejected suitor and her country's enemy but few pairs made their way to England.

"Where did you get the stockings?" asked Elizabeth with delight.

"Your Majesty," she answered, "I once saw a pair brought from Spain, and I made these expressly for your Grace."

"Can you get me more?" asked the queen eagerly.

"This very day," replied the silk-woman joyfully, "I will set up another pair, and knit more for your Grace."

"I'll wear no more stockings made of cloth," declared the queen. "These are pleasant and delicate. I mind me well that my father had two pairs, and by great chance there came a pair from Spain while my brother Edward was king. No more cloth hose for me, good Mistress Montague."

One of the queen's bold sea-captains presented her with a fan made of red and white feathers, "enameled with a half-moon of mother-of-pearl, within that a half-moon garnished with sparks of diamonds and a few seed pearls." A fan was once given to her by Leicester which was even more dazzling. It was made of white feathers; its handle was of gold; rubies, diamonds, and two superb emeralds were on one side; rubies, diamonds, and pearls were on the other. Leicester's coat of arms was a bear and ragged staff; therefore, there was a lion rampant with a white bear lying muzzled at its feet. A pair of gloves was in those days a fitting offering "to set before the queen." Handkerchiefs, a kind of nightdress that must have served as a wrapper, for it was of white linen embroidered with black and trimmed with lace and spangles, preserved ginger, lemons, pies, a purse of gold coins from a wealthy city or a piece of confectionery from her cook,—whatever came was welcome.

To live in splendor was the queen's paradise. Her books were bound in velvet, their clasps were of gold or of silver, and wherever there was space, the glitter of some precious stone flashed forth. Handsome furniture, fine tapestries, golden plate, were her joy. The trappings of her horses were superb; the harness was of gold and silk, the saddle was of black velvet embroidered with pearls and gold thread. It was valued at seven thousand dollars. Preparing her dinner table was an elaborate ceremonial. Each article of table use must be brought in by a servant preceded by an usher, and before it could be laid on the table, the servant must kneel three times. After it was put in place, the servant knelt once, and then the little procession returned for another article. When it was time for the food to be brought in, there was much more ceremony. Silken-clad lady tasters, tall yeomen of the guard, and eight maids of honor appeared. Drums and trumpets sounded, and then the food—rather cold, one would fancy—was borne in state to the chamber of the queen.

With all this love of magnificence Elizabeth had a thrifty notion of the value of economy in the adornments of others, and several times during her reign she had laws passed forbidding expensive attire. One of her proclamations stated that it caused "great inconvenience" to spend so much for dress, and that men were arraying their wives and children at so much "superfluous charge and expense" that they were no longer able to practise hospitality as they ought. "The lowest ought not to expect to dress as richly as their betters," declared the queen. "It is their pride that makes them rob and steal by the highway."

She even told her subjects just what materials they would be allowed to wear. Save for a few exceptions, ambassadors or commanders or Knights of the Garter, no one but an earl was allowed to wear purple silk or cloth of gold or of silver "tissued." No one below the rank of baron might dare to adorn himself with gold or silver lace, or wear a sword or rapier or dagger. The wife of a knight was permitted to appear in a velvet gown, cloak, or other upper garment, and she might embroider them with silk if she chose, but the wife of even a knight's eldest son could wear velvet only as a kirtle or petticoat. Her upper garment might be of satin, but she was forbidden to embroider it.

Elizabeth was not afraid to rebuke her ladies in waiting if their dress was too expensive to please her. One of them bought a velvet suit elaborately trimmed with gold and pearls. Elizabeth bore its appearance several times, then she had it brought to her secretly and put it on. Out among her ladies she went, wearing the elaborate gown, which was much too short for her. The owner of the velvet and pearls was aghast, but the queen smiled upon her and asked:—

"Think you not, Mistress Mary, that my gown is too short? Does it not become me ill?"

"Yes, your Majesty," faltered the poor lady.

"You are right," said the queen, "but mark you well that if it is too short for me, it is too fine for you." The gown never again appeared before the eyes of the queen.

CHAPTER XII

THE GREAT SEA-CAPTAINS

AS matters are looked at in these times, Elizabeth's relations to Spain were exceedingly strange. To-day if two countries are not at war, they are at peace, but in the sixteenth century it was not at all uncommon for two rulers to annoy each other as much as possible without any formal war, and more than once a third country joined one side or the other because in so doing there was an opportunity for gain.

Philip would have been glad to conquer England, but as long as Elizabeth maintained peace with France, there was little hope for him. Moreover, the Netherlands were keeping his hands full, and what was most exasperating, Elizabeth was helping the revolters. There was one more thing to be considered, if Philip did conquer England, there was no hope of his being able to claim the throne as long as Mary was alive. So it was that this ruler of half Europe, was really at the mercy of that exasperating monarch, Elizabeth of England, and she hectored and tormented him to her heart's content. Early in her reign most of her advisers would have been glad to go to war with Philip, but

Elizabeth delayed. She hated war. Every year of peace enriched and strengthened her kingdom, and moreover, even without fighting Philip, she was gaining much of the wealth and power that a Spanish conquest would have brought her.

This gain came about through the exploits of her sea-captains. As has been said before, it was regarded as an honorable occupation to get some negroes on the African coast, carry them to the Spanish colonies in America, and sell them for a goodly amount of Spanish gold. This was precisely what Sir John Hawkins did, but when he had leisurely made his way back to England, he found himself in trouble. Elizabeth sent for him.

"They tell me you are no better than a pirate," she said, bluntly, although her look was not so stern as Cecil would have wished.

"Your Majesty," replied Hawkins, "I am but a plain, simple sailor."

"And so my plain, simple sailors are bringing me into a war with King Philip?" asked Elizabeth.

Hawkins was no more afraid of the queen of England than of the king of Spain, and he told his own grievances as frankly as if she had been one of his men.

"Your Majesty," said he, "I took the blacks from the savage countries of Africa, and surely there was no harm in that. I carried them to Saint Domingo, and I sold them to the planters. The governor of the island was willing, and the planters were glad to get them. I paid the harbor dues, and I left one hundred negroes with him to pay a larger duty if the king asked more of an Englishman than he did of a Spaniard. I bought hides with the money and sent them in a Spanish vessel to be sold in Spain. The king seized them, and he won't pay me a penny for them."

"Well, my plain, simple sailor," asked the queen, "is it your will that I and my council should go to Spain and get your hides?"

"Your Majesty," he answered, "give me a good vessel under me and plenty of sea-room, and I'll trouble no council to care for me and my right." Elizabeth was in a rarely good-natured mood. She patted the captain on his broad shoulder.

"I'd gladly know what the king of Spain would do with such a saucy fellow as you," she said. "You'd better go home and think no more about the New World. One side of the Atlantic is enough for a man." The captain withdrew, but Elizabeth bade an attendant call him back.

"Let me understand when it is your will to go on another trip," she said, "for no one could expect a pirate to obey his queen, and then, too, I have a vessel that might be the better for a voyage or two, even in the hands of a simple sailor like yourself."

Cecil objected and the Spanish ambassador raged, but it was not long before Hawkins set out on another voyage, this time in a great ship of the queen's, and she as well as many of her council took shares in the enterprise. "See you to it that you do no wrong to the king of Spain," were the queen's orders, but she lent the commander one hundred good soldiers. When Hawkins came back in all the glory of a successful voyage and with bags of Spanish coins for queen and councilors, he was invited to dine with his sovereign. The Spanish ambassador was also dining at court, but he could have had little pleasure in his dinner, for he was thinking of what he should have to write to the king of Spain. What Philip said when the letters reached him no one knows, but whenever he came to the name of Hawkins, he wrote on the margin "Beware, beware!"

On one of Hawkins's voyages went a kinsman of his own named Francis Drake. He was a young man of medium height, with broad shoulders, reddish beard, and keen, kindly eyes. The voyage on which he went was unsuccessful, for a Spanish ship set upon the Englishmen and robbed them. Worse than that, there were not provisions enough to last on the trip home, and one hundred of his comrades volunteered to take their chances on the land that the rest of the company might be sure of safety.

Drake made up his mind that the king of Spain should pay for his own lost investment and his kinsman's captured hides to say nothing of reprisal for the suffering and perhaps death of the hundred brave men who had sacrificed themselves for their comrades. He did very little talking about his plans, but there were sailors enough in Plymouth who were ready to go anywhere with him, and he had friends who were willing to invest in any undertaking that he would lead. He set sail for America.

He was not going out vaguely into the west, hoping that somewhere he might pick up something worth bringing home, he had a very definite plan. He sailed straight for Panama and landed. There he waited. While he was waiting, he climbed a tall tree one day, and far to the westward the Pacific Ocean spread out before him. "If the almighty God will give me life," said he, "I'll sail a ship in those waters before many years."

After a while he and his men heard bits of Spanish song, the tinkling of bells on the necks of mules, and the sound of the feet of the animals striking upon the well-trodden path. Then the English dashed out, for this was King Philip's treasure train that once a year paced leisurely up the path with the output of the mines, with gold, silver, emeralds, and diamonds. There were more than the ship could carry, says the old story. The ship could easily come again, the ocean was free; so they buried the great bars of silver and steered for England.

When Drake arrived, he made no boast of what he had done, he divided the treasure and did no talking. He read books on geography, he studied charts and globes, he questioned seamen who had been on the farther side of the ocean, and he had more than one interview with the queen and different members of her council. To agree as a council to support Drake would be to declare war against Spain, and it would not answer to have the names of the councilors who invested in the enterprise made public, but many a one among them, and even the queen herself was ready to fill a coffer or two with good Spanish gold.

The preparations were so unusual that the voyage could not be kept secret. "I pray your Majesty," wrote the Spanish ambassador to Philip, "I pray you order your planters in the New World to hang every Englishman upon whom they can lay hands, and bid your sailors sink every ship that comes in their sight."

The two vessels, one of one hundred and twenty tons and one of eighty tons, with three little sloops, were made ready. Everything about them was put in the best order possible for fighting or for sailing. Luxuries were not forgotten, for this keen young sailor did not scorn the elegancies of life. There was handsome furniture finely carved. There was a beautiful silver service for his table, every piece engraved with the arms of his family. His cooking utensils were of silver. He had a liberal supply of perfumes, many of them the gift of the queen. Expert musicians were on board, for this luxurious captain must dine and sup to the sound of music.

With his men he was ever kindly, even affectionate, and he was not afraid to share their work if there was need, but they knew him for one that could command, and they never failed in their respect. Nine or ten men formed his council. He decided all questions himself, but he ever listened attentively to what they had to say. They dined at his table, but not one of them ventured to be seated in his presence or to wear a hat without the invitation of their commander. November 15, 1577, the little fleet set sail at five o'clock in the afternoon—on a one day's voyage it proved for the *Golden Hind*, Drake's own ship, was injured in the "forcible storm and tempests" that arose, and he had to go back to land.

Three years later many a man in England was troubled about the deeds of this commander who was so fond of perfumes and music and silver plate, for there were stories abroad of what he had done on the other side of the sea. Philip was furious; the Spanish ambassador raged, and more than one who had invested in Drake's venture every shilling that he could raise would have rejoiced to lose his money if he could have been sure that Drake would never return. In the midst of the anxiety and uncertainty, some eager to have him come in safely and others trembling at the thought of his arrival, there was a mighty roaring of the signal guns at Plymouth Harbor, for Drake had returned, and he had been around the world.

On a little hill, somewhat withdrawn from the crowd that stood shouting and cheering to see the ship come in, stood two men, the elder grave and troubled, the younger eager and excited.

"I verily believe," said the elder, "that you would willingly be among those doltish screamers on the shore yonder."

"It's not so bad a thing, is it, for a man to know that his money has come back to him doubled ten, twelve, perhaps a hundred times? It's little wonder that they scream."

"That goes as it may," returned the elder, "but the gold in that vessel is devil's gold. If half the tales be true, Francis Drake is no better than a pirate. Has he not burned settlements, stolen treasure, and sunk galleons?"

"Well, what of it, if they be those of Spain?" asked the young man indifferently, shading his eyes to see the ships more clearly.

"Nothing of it if a man cares for naught but gold, nothing of it to him whose empty money-bags are a sorer grief to him than the ill that is sure to come to England from this wild and savage piracy."

"You mean that old leaden foot will bestir himself?"

"Philip is slow, but he will strike at last."

"Let him. One Englishman can meet two Spaniards any day."

"He boasts best who boasts last," said the elder. "Remember that every Spaniard has his hands full of gold from the American mines."

"And it is you yourself who are blaming Captain Drake for taking it from them," laughed the young fellow gaily. "Goodby, uncle, I'm going down among the wicked folk to see the ships come to shore."

For once the stories were not equal to the reality. In the holds of Drake's vessels were such masses of treasure that men hardly ventured even to estimate it. Vast quantities were carried to the Tower of London. Drake made most costly gifts to the nobles, but some of them refused to accept anything from the "master thief of the unknown world," as they called him.

"He is nothing but a robber," declared they, "and he will bring war upon us."

"Is it robbery, demanded others, to take from Spain what Spain has stolen from us? How else can a man get his rights? Has not Philip taken our ships, hindered our commerce, captured our sailors, and tortured them to make them give up the true faith? Have we not a clear right to take reprisal when and where we can?"

"It is a lawful prize," reasoned others, "and if war is to come, this Spanish gold will save taxes and fight many a battle for us."

The Spanish ambassador went straight to the queen and said gravely, "I present from my master, the king of Spain, a request that the pirate Drake be surrendered to him."

"The king of Spain is generous with his presents," answered Elizabeth flippantly. "For this one I return him all due thanks."

"Your Majesty," said the ambassador, "this man Drake has sunk our ships, stolen our treasure, and interfered with our possessions in the New World."

"If you can prove his misdeeds to my satisfaction," rejoined the queen with a little yawn, "this wonderful treasure of yours shall be restored, though one might think it was but fair payment for the rebellions that Spain has caused in Ireland—or does my good friend Philip claim Ireland too for his own? As for his possessions in the New World, I don't know what right the Pope has to give away continents. The sea and the air are free to all, and neither Pope nor Spain can keep my brave captains from sailing the ocean, I doubt whether I could keep them from it myself. Shall we talk of other matters? You have an excellent taste in music, and here is a rare bit of song that has but newly come to me:—

> " 'The little pretty nightingale
>   Among the leaves green—' "

"Your Majesty," broke in the exasperated ambassador, "if I report this scene to King Philip, matters will come to the cannon."

"You really shouldn't say such things," said Elizabeth with a coquettish glance at the enraged Spaniard, and she added quietly, "If you do, I shall have to throw you into one of my dungeons."

Elizabeth made Drake a knight, she wore his jewels in her crown, and she dined with him on board the *Golden Hind*. She often had him at court, and never wearied of hearing the story of his adventures.

"Tell me of the savages," she commanded, and Drake began:—

"We saw them moving about under the trees, and when we came near, they paddled out to meet us. They made a long speech with many gestures, and it seemed as if they couldn't do us reverence enough. The next day they came again, and this time they brought a great ragged bunch of crow's feathers. The man who stood at the king's right hand knelt before me and touched the ground with his forehead three times. Then he gave me the feathers. I noticed that the king's guards all wore such bunches on their heads, so I stuck them in my red cap as well as ever I could, and the savages all danced around me and made the most unearthly screeching that I ever heard. Then they began to show us their wounds and sores, and made signs that we should blow on them to heal them. I gave them plasters and lotions. They ought to do some good, for they were mixed on a day that Dr. Dee said would make any medicine of worth."

"Tell me about the *Cacafuego*," bade the queen, and Drake said:—

"We took a Spanish ship, and one of the sailors said, 'Let me go free and I will tell you such news as you never heard before.' I promised, and he said, 'There's a ship not far ahead of you, her name is the *Cacafuego*, and if you can catch her, you'll have such a prize as you never saw in a dream—and I'll get my revenge on her captain for this,' he muttered, and then he put his hand on a great red scar on his forehead. We chased her to Payta, but she had gone to Panama, and when we came to Panama, she was somewhere else. 'I'll give a gold chain to the first man that sees her,' I said, and, your Majesty, if I had even given an order to drop anchor, I verily believe every man of them would have climbed the masthead. Well, about three o'clock one afternoon my page John caught sight of her, and we pursued. Oh, but it was glorious! I wish you had been there!" said the sturdy sailor, forgetting for a moment that he was addressing the sovereign of England.

"So do I," declared Elizabeth, and she too forgot that she was a queen, she forgot everything but the wild adventures that the man before her had met. Drake went on:—

"We fired across her bow, but she wouldn't stop. Then we shot three pieces of ordnance and struck down her mizzen mast, and we boarded her. A man could wade up to his waist in the treasure in her hold. There were thirteen chests full of Spanish reals, there were six and twenty tons of silver, and fourscore pounds of gold, and there were jewels and precious stones. Your Majesty can see them in the Tower, but oh, how they glittered and flashed and sparkled in the dark hold of the vessel when we broke open the caskets and turned the light of the lanterns on them, and how the dons swore at us! It's many a month that they should do penance for that day's work."

"I really wonder that you didn't excommunicate them as you did your own chaplain," said Elizabeth.

"They were only swearing, and he was a coward," explained Drake. "A man who'll go about among the sailors before a fight and tell them he is not sure that it is the will of God to give them the victory ought to be excommunicated, he ought to be hanged."

"Tell me again just what you said," demanded the queen, "that I may see what penalty you deserve for daring to show dishonor to one of my chaplains."

"I chained him by the leg to the forehatch," replied Drake, "and I said, 'Francis Fletcher, I do here excommunicate thee out of the church of God, and I renounce thee to the devil and all his angels;' and then I tied a riband around his arm, and I said, 'If so be that you dare to unbind this riband, you'll swing from that yardarm as sure as my name is Francis Drake.' "

"And what was it you wrote on the riband?" asked the queen, though well knowing the answer.

"I wrote 'Francis Fletcher, the falsest knave that liveth.' I don't see how I could have done less."

"Neither do I," agreed Elizabeth heartily, "and it would but ill become me to differ with a man who has just given me a New Albion. Where say you that my new domain lies?"

"On the western shores of North America," answered Drake, "and perchance, your Majesty, this new domain may stretch into Asia itself, for the western land reaches much farther west than I had thought, and it may be that in the far north the New World touches the old."

"Then I am perhaps queen of the Indies," said Elizabeth with a smile. "Now go, my brave sailor, but see to it that you come soon to court again, for there is much more that I would know of this wicked journey of yours."

So it was that these bold buccaneers went on their voyages, not so much for adventure or discovery as for the sake of gold. The easiest way to get gold was to take it from the Spanish settlements in America, but when Drake sailed, the Spaniards on the eastern coast of America were becoming wary. Too many of their treasure ships had been attacked and too many of their settlements robbed for them to live as carelessly as had been the case in the earlier days. Spanish ships on the Atlantic were manned with men who could fight, and Spanish settlements on the eastern coast of America were guarded and fortified.

On the Pacific shore matters were different. Spanish gold from the fabulously rich mines of Peru was carried leisurely up the coast in vessels manned chiefly by negro slaves. At Panama it was unloaded and taken across the isthmus. Then it was carefully guarded, and vessels well supplied with Spanish troops bore it across the ocean to the treasure vaults of Philip. It did not occur to the Spaniards that even an English corsair would venture to round Cape Horn, and when Drake appeared among the unprotected ships and the unfortified settlements, he found an easy prey. It was less dangerous for him to cross the Pacific and double the Cape of Good Hope than to return to England among the Spanish vessels on the Atlantic; and that is why Drake was the first Englishman to sail around the world.

These English buccaneers sailed under a sort of roving commission from the queen. They were to give her a share of their profits, but they knew well that if they could not extricate themselves from any trouble that they might fall into with Philip, she would make no effort to defend them, but would declare that they had had orders to do no harm to her "good friend, the king of Spain." Still, the prizes of success were so enormous and the charm of adventure so enticing that there was no lack of bold leaders to rob the coffers of Spain, to fill the treasury of Elizabeth, and to prepare experienced seamen for the great struggle that awaited England when Philip "of the leaden foot" should at last arise and show his might.

CHAPTER XIII

THE NEW WORLD

T O most of the sailors of Elizabeth's time the chief inducement to make a voyage to the westward lay in the possibility of winning Spanish gold in one way or another, but a few sailed with quite a different object. A little more than a century before Drake's famous voyage around the world, Columbus had crossed the Atlantic, hoping to find a shorter passage to India. In the days of Elizabeth it was well known that a continent blocked the way to Asia, but mariners had no idea that North America was nearly as broad as it has proved to be, and they were ever hoping to find a passage through it to the wonderful countries of spices and gems and perfumes.

Interest in the New World was increasing. Every year new maps, books of travel, and descriptions of various parts of the earth, especially of America, were published, some of the descriptions real and some almost wholly imaginative; but whatever they were, they always found readers.

One man who watched eagerly for whatever came from the press about the New World was a sea-captain named Martin Frobisher. He read all these books, he studied globes and charts, and at last he felt sure that he knew the way to fame and wealth, but he was a poor man and he could not carry out his plans alone. He sought an audience with the queen.

"I've heard of you before, my gallant captain," said Elizabeth graciously. "Didn't you care for the building of one of my ships that were sent against the Irish rebels?"

"I did, your Majesty, and if only that ship belonged to me, I would put her to a noble use."

"And what might that be?" asked the queen.

"Your Majesty, men have sailed to the northeast, to the south, and to the west, but no man has yet gone to the north of the New World. There lies the way to India, and to find that way is the only thing in all the world that is yet left undone whereby a man may become both rich and notable."

"And so you plan to go to the northwest?" asked Elizabeth.

"He who has little gold must have few plans, but it might well be that as the southern land tapers to a point, so the northern land narrows, and then with an open sea and a short voyage to Cathay, what would the wealth of the Spanish mines be to us? We could buy and sell in every clime. Give us the riches of India, and we could fit out a fleet that would drive King Philip from the shores of the New World, from the waters of the Atlantic, from——"

"Perchance from the face of the earth, my captain?" interrupted Elizabeth. "I promise you that I will think of this scheme of yours."

Elizabeth did think of it, but to her mind there was a far greater charm in a wild voyage of buccaneering than in the possibilities of slow gain by trading with people across two oceans, and she gave Frobisher no help. He won a friend, however, in the Earl of Warwick, and the fleet of three daring little vessels set out for the north. Elizabeth did not help to pay the costs of the voyage, but she stood on the shore and waved her royal hand to the commander as he dropped slowly down the Thames.

Frobisher came home with great joy. He had entered the strait that is called after him, and he had seen, as he believed, America lying on his left hand and Asia on his right. That was surely the way to India. It is no wonder that crowds went to visit his tiny barque.

"Can you not give me a memento of the voyage?" asked a lady.

"Next year I will bring you a memento from China," answered Frobisher. "Shall it be silks or jewels or perfumes?"

"Beggars should not be choosers," said the lady with a smile, "but give me a bit of this strange black stone as a pledge that you will not forget me next year when you are even more famous than you are to-day."

"One of the sailors brought that aboard," said Frobisher. "It looks like sea-coal, but it is as heavy as iron."

This little gift put Frobisher at the head of a fleet of fifteen vessels, but he was no longer free to win glory as an explorer. The bit of black stone was dropped into the fire to see whether it would burn, and then vinegar was poured upon it. It glittered, and an Italian chemist declared that it was rich in gold. After this there was no difficulty in raising funds for a voyage to the marvelous country of the north where gold lay about on the surface of the ground.

The ships sailed, but they met icebergs, fog, and storm. Frobisher hesitated. He believed that he could force his way to the Pacific, but his orders were to make sure of the gold, and he loaded his ships with what proved to be only worthless earth. In later years he won honors and wealth, but his dream of finding the Northwest Passage was never realized.

Thus far most people had thought of America as a place where a man might be fortunate enough to find a gold mine, but where he was quite as likely to be killed by the Indians or captured by the Spaniards. Others looked upon it as a troublesome mass of land that blocked the way to the riches of commerce with India. To one young courtier this strange New World was something more than the home of possible gold mines, and in his mind it was certainly not an obstacle to wealth and success. This young man was named Walter Raleigh. He had shown his scholarship at Oxford and his bravery in a campaign in Ireland. It came to pass that he and the lord deputy of Ireland disagreed. "I wish to defend myself before the royal council," said Raleigh. This defence was managed so skilfully that the queen listened with the closest attention.

"Bring that young Raleigh to me," she commanded when the council dissolved.

Raleigh knelt before her and kissed her hand.

"Young man," said she, "you seem to have been in no way worsted by those mighty councilors of mine."

"Your Majesty," answered Raleigh with the look of admiration that was so dear to Elizabeth, "could one fail to be aroused to the best that is in him when he has the honor of speaking in the glorious presence of his sovereign?"

"What can you do?" asked the queen bluntly, but most graciously, for this kind of flattery was ever a delight to her.

"Shall I bring from Ireland the bodies of those who have dared to rebel against your Majesty's wise and gentle rule?" asked Raleigh, "that they may testify of me?"

"You can fight. Can you do aught beside?"

"Truly, yes, I can count myself the happiest and most favored of mortals in that upon me is turned the kindly thought of her who surpasseth all other women as far as the glowing sun doth surpass the beams of the farthing rushlight."

Raleigh was wise enough to keep the favor that he had won. Elizabeth could rebuke a maid of honor for wearing too expensive a gown, but of her courtiers she demanded the most handsome attire that their purses could provide. This new favorite had only a shallow purse, but he willingly spent every penny that he could raise on brilliant apparel, and he neglected no opportunity to make himself of use to the queen.

One morning the rain was falling fast, and one of the ladies in waiting said:—

"Surely your Majesty will remain indoors to-day."

"My servants may dread the raindrops," answered Elizabeth, "but a queen should fear nothing."

"With two thousand gowns she may well afford to spoil one for every shower," said one lady to another. This was before the days of umbrellas, but there was nothing to do save to hope for sunshine. The hour for the walk came, and the queen went forth. The sun had come out.

"Someone has been praying for clear skies," said she, "and verily I wish he had broadened his prayer a bit and prayed also for dry ground."

"It must have been young Raleigh," said one of the ladies to another a little pointedly. "He loves to dwell in the sunshine as the moth loves the beam of the candle."

"There isn't another man in England who can tell just what to do in any difficulty as well as he," declared another lady.

"Then I would that he were here now," whispered the first. "The queen will go straight across that miry place, and if she is ill, we shall have to bear the blame."

"There he comes as if he had been sent for," said the second, for Raleigh was approaching. He was decked out in the bravest attire and was daintily picking his way along the muddy road.

"It's but this day week that he had a new scarlet cloak," said a lady in the train, "and see the gorgeousness of the blue plush that he wears this morning! I'll warrant he put his last shilling into it."

The queen hesitated a moment, but there was no hesitation in Raleigh. Quick as thought, he slipped off the shining blue plush mantle and spread it on the ground before Elizabeth.

"She who is to her devoted people the glory of the sunlight must never fail to see under her feet the reflection of that clear sky which her shining has bestowed upon her fortunate subjects." So said the courtier, and he well knew that in the glance of approval given him by Elizabeth lay the promise of many cloaks.

He rose rapidly in the queen's favor. She gave him whatever he asked, and he did not hesitate to ask for what he wanted. Elizabeth had a fashion of rewarding a favorite by giving him a "monopoly," as it was called, that is, the sole right to sell some one thing. One man had the right to sell gunpowder, another salt, while yet another was the only man in England who was allowed to collect and export old shoes. To Raleigh she gave the privilege of exporting woolen cloth, and at another time the sole right to sell wine in the kingdom. He was no longer a poor young courtier, straining every resource to dress as handsomely as the taste of the queen demanded. Now he wore silver armor that sparkled with rubies and pearls and diamonds. Even his shoes were so encrusted with jewels that they were said to be worth more than six thousand gold pieces. Money flowed freely into his coffers. Besides Elizabeth's other gifts, he could ask for his monopolies whatever price he chose, and whoever wished to buy must pay it. There were rumors that this brilliant young favorite had higher aspirations, even to the hand of the queen herself. The story is told that one day when Raleigh was standing by a window, tracing idly scrolls and letters on the pane with a diamond, he heard the queen coming up softly behind him. He went on as if he did not know of her presence and wrote on the glass:—

"Fain would I climb, but that I fear to fall."

Elizabeth drew a diamond ring from her finger and put an ending to the couplet:—

"If thy heart fail thee, do not climb at all."

With such encouragement, it is no wonder that Raleigh felt sure of her interest in whatever he wished to attempt. He had a great undertaking in mind, and between his compliments to Elizabeth his thoughts often turned to the westward, to the wonderful New World. It was not hard to persuade the queen to give him a grant of land in America, and he sent out two barques to explore the coast north of Florida. When the skippers returned, Raleigh brought them before the queen.

"Is this new country so much better than our own old England?" she asked.

"Nothing could be better than the land which has the happiness to be ruled directly by your Majesty," answered Raleigh, "but, truly, the New World is a goodly place."

"How does it differ from our land?" asked the queen of one of the skippers, and he answered:—

"Your Majesty, as we drew near the shore, there was no smell of wharfs or fishing, but a fragrance as if we were in the midst of some delicate garden."

"We have perfumes in England," said the queen. "Did you discover anything better than pleasant odors?" she asked of the second skipper.

"Yes, your Majesty, we found what is not in all England, for when we landed, the low, sandy shore was so overgrown with grapes that the very beating and surge of the sea overflowed them; the vines ran over hills and plains, they climbed every little shrub, and they made their way to the tops of the cedars. I do think that in all the world the like abundance is not to be found."

"Perfumes and grapes," said the queen. "Raleigh, my man, that is a good beginning. Send your skippers away, and tell me what is your request, for I know you have one. When will you ever cease begging, Walter?"

"When you cease to be so kind a benefactress," was the courtier's shrewd and graceful reply.

The skippers were sent away, and the queen said:—

"Now tell me about this land of grapes. Fruit and perfumes are well enough, but they do little to fill an empty treasury. What else lies within your patent?"

"There are beasts of all kinds that roam the forests, there are birds and fish, there are the highest and reddest cedars of the world, coral of red and white, pearls, fruits, vegetables, natives that are gentle and kindly and void of all guile and treason."

"What do you call this paradise of yours?"

"The natives call it Wingina."

"I'll give you a better name. It was visited while a virgin queen was on the throne, so call it Virginia, and I'll be its godmother."

"O, Madam," said Raleigh with enthusiasm, "never had a sovereign such a chance to add to the glory of her renown. America is not only a country in which one may make a fortune, it is a fortune in itself. Why should it not become a second home of the English nation?"

The queen's eyes kindled. "How could that be?" she asked.

"Your Majesty," he answered, eagerly, "the soil of Virginia is the richest in the world. The natives sow their corn in May and they reap it in July; they sow it again in June and July, and they reap it but two months after the planting. Our men put peas into the ground, and in ten days they were fourteen inches high. Beans and wheat and oats may be had for the asking."

"And supposing my good friend Philip should fall upon these amazingly fertile lands, he might put the colonists to the sword even before their peas were above the ground."

"Might we not also fancy a strong band of colonists building vessels of the goodly trees of the Virginia forests and sailing out boldly into the Atlantic to capture the treasure ships of Spain? Might not the colonists steer to the northward and free our Newfoundland fishing grounds from the hateful presence of the Spaniard?"

" 'Walter, thou reasonest well,' " laughed the queen, "but one little thing you've mayhap forgot. Tell me, Walter, my man, where shall we find these worthy colonists who are to raise corn in two months and fight King Philip while it is growing?"

"Your Majesty," answered the courtier gravely, "those who are driven from England will be our colonists."

"Driven from England," repeated the queen, "what mean you by that?"

"Our farmers have long been raising sheep instead of grain," said he. "One man can easily care for many sheep. Those men that are driven from their old farm work can find naught else to do. They must starve or steal, and, Madam, it grieves me sorely to see that twenty or even thirty are often hanged before the hour of noon for stealing a shilling or perchance but a morsel of bread."

"They who steal must be punished," said the queen, "but it would please me well if there were some other remedy than hanging."

"The corn of Virginia will be a remedy, my queen, and there is yet another benefit that would come to England from colonies across the Atlantic. We wish to spread our commerce to foreign lands, but if we have a second England on the other side of the sea, will not our own countrymen of America buy and sell with us? Cannot laws be made that they shall trade with no others, if, indeed, they should be so disloyal as to think of such a thing? Why need we care for trade with a nation across the Pacific when we can trade with our own people in Virginia?"

"Walter, you are wonderfully in earnest about this scheme of yours. It would ill become me to question the fairness or worthiness of my godchild, and I will think of what you say, I will think of it."

Elizabeth thought of the plan, indeed the air was so full of talk about the proposed Virginian colony that she could have hardly helped thinking about it. In Virginia there was fertile soil, a good hope of finding gems and gold, and little probability of trouble with the Indians. Her councilors discussed the plan. Said one to another:—

"Think you that the queen will aid young Raleigh?"

" 'Sir Walter' you must say now that he has become a knight," rejoined the second. "Yes, I do believe that she will. Has she not followed his every whim till Leicester has fairly turned green with jealousy? She has just given him the wine monopoly, and that is worth thousands of pounds in a single year. If she gives him that, would she withhold aid for the bringing up of this 'godchild' of hers?"

"You're a shrewd man, I admit," said the first, "but I've watched this queen of ours since she was no higher than my table, and I've never yet seen her affection for any one get the better of her. She's a woman, but she's also a queen, and she's more queen than woman."

"I'm not the man to hold an opinion and fear to back it up," rejoined the other. "I've a fair bit of land down in Devon, and I'll wager it against that house of yours in London that she'll help 'educate the godchild.' "

The land was lost, for Elizabeth could not bear to part with her gold pieces unless she could be sure of a generous return. Raleigh did not give up his plan, however, and soon a company of colonists was sent to Roanoke Island, off the coast of what is now North Carolina. The colony failed because the new settlers were too eager to search for gold to spend their time planting corn and beans, or even peas that would grow fourteen inches in ten days. "They are lazy and homesick, and they talk too much," reported the governor, and when a fleet of Drake's came to shore, they all went aboard and sailed for home.

These homesick colonists carried tobacco with them to England, and smoking soon became the fashionable amusement. Sir Walter was enthusiastic in its praise.

"One would think that this wonderful plant of yours was your own child," said the queen to him as he sat puffing out the smoke from his silver pipe, "you claim for it so many virtues."

"You say well, Madam," declared Sir Walter. "It is verily a wonderful plant."

"And I suppose you would even say that you could tell the weight of that smoke of yours. There's no boundary to your impudence."

"Indeed I can, your Majesty," returned Sir Walter calmly.

"I'll wager this pin against your buckle that you cannot," retorted the queen.

"I'll take the wager," said he, "and with the more joy since the experiment will secure me the delight of your presence." He weighed some tobacco and put it into his pipe. Then after he had smoked it he weighed the ashes. "The difference is the weight of the smoke," said he, and Elizabeth paid the bet. "Many a man have I known who has turned his gold into smoke," she declared merrily, "but you are surely the first who has turned his smoke into gold. You're a marvelous man, Sir Walter."

CHAPTER XIV

THE QUEEN OF SCOTS

THE councilor's words that Elizabeth was more queen than woman were shown to be true whenever matters came to the proof. She gave her favorite Leicester everything that he asked save her own royal hand, but on occasion she could be as severe with Leicester as if he had been her enemy.

It was the custom for the general of an English army to serve without salary and to contribute generously to his own expenses and those of his troops. The general, then, must be a rich man, and in order to have the most perfect control over his soldiers he must be a man who was known to be in the confidence of the queen. No one was better qualified in these important respects to lead an army than Leicester, and he was put at the head of the forces that were sent to the aid of the Dutch states then revolting against Philip. Their leader had been assassinated, and they asked to be annexed to England. Elizabeth saw clearly that to grant their request would bring on war with Spain at once, and she refused. When Leicester was appointed commander, she gave him the most positive orders to accept no such position for her as ruler of the Low

Countries. News soon came that Leicester had been made governor general.

"Your Majesty," said her informer, "it is said that Lord Leicester is shown great honor in the Low Countries."

"That is well," said the queen. "The commander of an army should ever be treated with deference."

"The Dutch states prove by the respect given to Lord Leicester what honor they would show to your Majesty if you were with them."

"In what fashion do they show their respect?" asked the queen so gently that Leicester's enemy took courage and ventured to go a step further.

"He is called governor-general, and they say that men kneel before him to kiss his hand, and that he has already a court as brilliant as that of England."

"Is that true?" asked Elizabeth with a feigned indifference. "Do you know more of this court of his?"

"Little now, but there will be more and greater news, for it is said that Lady Leicester is about to go to Holland and that with her will go such a train of ladies and gentlemen and such rich coaches, litters, and side-saddles, that your Majesty has none such in England."

Then Elizabeth's wrath broke forth. "I will let the upstart know," said she, "how easily the hand that has exalted him can beat him down." She wrote an angry letter to her absent favorite which said:—

"I have raised you from the dust and shown you favor above all others, and I should never have imagined you would dare to break my express commandment to accept any such title."

It was a hard position for Burleigh, since he himself and the rest of the council had wished Leicester to accept the title and so force the queen to become sovereign of the Dutch states, whether she would or not. The queen's rage was visited upon even her old friend and adviser, and to Burleigh himself she declared, "You are nothing but a presumptuous fellow."

The great test of Elizabeth's character was soon to come, for the year 1587 was at hand. Would she be woman or queen? A stern question must be decided. Jesting with Raleigh, exasperating King Philip, storming at Leicester and then forgiving him, amusing herself with Leicester's handsome stepson, the Earl of Essex, bedecking herself in gorgeous attire that flashed with jewels and gold, dreaming over new routes to India and new English nations in Virginia—all these had to be put away for the time. What should be the fate of the Queen of Scots could no longer be left undecided.

Mary had been a captive in England for nearly eighteen years, and those years had been almost as full of peril to Elizabeth as to her prisoner. If Mary was dead, the Catholics who were plotting against Elizabeth would have no object in trying to take her life, for Mary's son James was the next heir to the throne, and he was as strong a Protestant as Elizabeth. On the other hand, if Elizabeth were no longer alive, Mary would become queen of England, and Protestants would be obliged to be loyal to her as their lawful sovereign. They would be the more content knowing that her Protestant son would succeed her. Thus, if either Mary or Elizabeth were dead, England would be free from the plots and conspiracies that had been revealed, one after another, during the captivity of Mary.

At the discovery of each of these plots, Mary's imprisonment became more rigorous. It was claimed that she was at the bottom of every conspiracy.

"The Queen of Scots and her friends will yet have my life," said Elizabeth, and she added jestingly to her councilors, "I'll come back after I am dead and see her make your heads fly."

Walsingham, one of Elizabeth's ministers, had been most watchful of these plots. His spies were ever on the lookout, and in the summer of 1586 he found sure proof of a conspiracy to take the life of the queen. Was Mary connected with this plot? Sworn testimony declared that she was. Her papers were seized, and among them were found letters from many leading nobles of England expressing sympathy in her troubles. Mary was at once removed to Fotheringay Castle, where she was much more closely guarded than ever before. Thirty-six commissioners were appointed to try her on the charge of plotting against the life of the English queen. She was cited to appear before them.

"That will I never do," she declared. "I have a right to be tried by my peers. I am a queen, and only sovereigns are my peers, but I will defend myself before the queen of England and her council or even before the English Parliament."

Then a letter was given her from Elizabeth which read:—

"You have attempted to take my life and to bring my kingdom to destruction by bloodshed. I have never proceeded so harshly against you, but have protected and maintained you like myself. It is my will that you answer the nobles and peers of the kingdom as if I were myself present. Act plainly, without reserve, and you will sooner be able to obtain favor from me."

"Is it wise to make these refusals?" asked one of her friends. "You are in the power of the English queen, is it not better to rouse her no further by hopeless demands?"

"True, it is hopeless," answered Mary, "it is all hopeless. I am a sovereign kept here unlawfully as a prisoner by the royal cousin to whom I fled for help in my trouble. Her laws have not protected me, why then must I be sentenced under them?"

"The court is convened," said the commissioners, "and if you refuse to appear, you will be at once declared guilty without a trial. Queen Elizabeth has said many times that nothing would please her so much as to have proof of your innocence. Is it wise to refuse to give proof?"

Finally Mary yielded. Her trial would not be legal to-day, for she was allowed no counsel, she was not even permitted to see her own papers or to hear and question those persons who testified against her, but it was according to the laws of the time, and she was tried with no greater severity than was shown to all prisoners accused of treason.

"Your letters prove that you have allowed your correspondents to address you as queen of England," declared the crown lawyers, "that you have tried to induce King Philip to invade our country, and that you have been knowing to the late plot to assassinate the lawful queen of the realm."

"With the plot against the life of my cousin Elizabeth I had nothing to do," declared Mary. "That I have sought to gain my freedom by the aid of my friends I do not deny. My lords, I am unjustly and cruelly deprived of my liberty. Do you blame me for trying by every means in my power to recover it? Could anyone do otherwise?"

So the charges and the denials went on, and when the trial was over, the judges left Fotheringay Castle. Again they met, and everyone voted that Mary was guilty of high treason in plotting against the life of the English queen. She was sentenced to death. This was the report made to Parliament, and that body solemnly agreed to the verdict. It was proclaimed in London, and the whole city gave itself up to rejoicing. Bells were rung, bonfires blazed in every square, shouts of joy and psalms of thanksgiving resounded throughout the town.

"Think you that the queen will ever carry out the sentence?" asked one Londoner of another.

Mary Stuart receiving her death sentence.—*From painting by Carl Piloty.*

"It is many years," was the reply, "that the hand of Elizabeth alone has saved the life of the Scotch queen. Parliament decreed her death fifteen years ago and they say that Elizabeth was the angriest woman in England. 'Would you have me put to death the bird that, to escape the hawk, has fled to me for protection? I'll never sign such a bill,' and she never did."

"The constant dropping of water will wear away stone," said the first, "and yet I hear that she has sent a message to Parliament commanding them to find some other way."

"Until the axe falls, nothing will persuade me that the child of Henry VIII. will consent to see the blood of one of her own proud race flow at the hand of the executioner," declared the second, "and what is more, she will not do a deed that will arouse the scorn and hatred of Europe. Mary's head is safe."

"Not so fast, my friend. Who are the supporters of Mary? Who is the 'Europe' whose scorn will check the pen of Elizabeth when she is about to sign the death warrant?"

"Philip, the Pope, the king of France, and Mary's own son James. They are a powerful company."

"Are they? Philip is really almost at war with us now, but it is not in Mary's interest. The Pope cares nothing about putting a Catholic woman of forty-four on the throne when in a few years she will be succeeded by a Protestant son. The king of France can do nothing for her but plead, for if he strikes one blow at England, it is a blow in favor of Spain."

"Her own son—"

"Has made a treaty with Elizabeth. He will do anything to make sure of the English throne, and indeed, can he be blamed for lack of affection when he knows that his mother planned to leave her claim not to him but to Philip?"

Elizabeth was most unwilling that Mary should be put to death. Her ministers were eager for the execution, for it was their business to secure the peace of England and the welfare of their queen. They believed that only Mary's death would bring this about. Then, too, as Elizabeth had said jestingly, if Mary were once on the throne, she would "make their heads fly."

Surely they had a right to care for their own safety, they reasoned. Elizabeth could not bear the thought that a princess of the Tudor blood should die on the scaffold. She was always careless of her personal danger, and she knew that the death of Mary would be ascribed to her own fear or jealousy. It is no wonder that she hesitated.

"What shall we do," queried the ministers. "Elizabeth must be induced to sign the death warrant, of course, but who will order it carried out?"

"The queen will never do such a thing," said one.

"We must do it ourselves," said another. "There are ten of us, and ten cannot well be made to suffer for carrying out a written order of the queen's."

For many weeks Elizabeth hesitated. She often sat buried in deep thought. "Shall I bear with her or smite her?" the ladies of the bed-chamber heard her say to herself. At last she bade the secretary Davison bring her the warrant.

"What have you in your hand?" she asked as he entered the room.

"Sundry papers that await your Majesty's signature," answered Davison. Elizabeth took up her pen and signed the warrant. Then she pushed it away from her and it fell upon the floor.

"Are you not heartily sorry to see this done?" she asked.

Elizabeth signing the death warrant of Mary Stuart—*From painting by Liezen-Mayer.*

"I should be far from rejoicing in any one's calamity," replied Davison, "but the life of the Queen of Scots is so great a threat to the life of your Majesty that not to sign the paper would be a wrong to your whole realm as much as to yourself."

"I have done all that either law or reason could require of me," said the queen, "and now let me hear nothing further."

Davison reported the scene to the council.

"She means the deed to be done," said one, "but she has given no orders to carry out the warrant."

"That is her way of dealing with her sea-captains," said another. "Does she not provide them with ships and guns and soldiers, and does she not most willingly take a share of Spanish gold? But if a commander gets into trouble with Spain, she will say, 'Did I not give orders to do no harm to my good friend Philip?'"

"Then must all ten of us give the final order," said another. This was done. The warrant and the letter commanding the execution were sent.

About a week after the signing of the warrant, bonfires blazed and bells rang.

"The bells ring as merrily as if there were some good news," said the queen. "Why is it?"

"It is because of the death of the Queen of Scots," was the answer. Elizabeth said not a word. A day or two later she was told that Mary had been executed at Fotheringay Castle. She turned pale, she burst into tears, she stormed at her councilors. "Never shall your crime be pardoned," she raged. "You well knew that I did not mean my kinswoman to be put to death. You have dared to usurp my authority, and you are worse traitors than my poor cousin. As for you, Burleigh, do you never dare show yourself in my presence again. I have made you and I can unmake you. That fellow Davison knew that I did not mean the warrant to be carried out. Take him to the Tower."

"He is very ill, your Majesty," said one.

"Then take his illness with him, for into the Tower he goes."

"Your Majesty," pleaded the councilors, "if your secretary Davison is imprisoned, the lords of your council will be regarded as plotters and murderers."

"What is that to me?" cried Elizabeth. "They who murder must expect to be called murderers."

Davison was imprisoned for some time and was fined so heavily that he was reduced to poverty. Elizabeth sent a copy of his sentence to King James and also a letter telling him that the execution of his mother was a "miserable accident." James was easily comforted. He had been taught to look upon her as a shame and disgrace to himself. If she had not been the murderer of his father, she had, at least, married the murderer, and within three months after the commission of the crime. He was lawful heir to the throne of England, but he knew that she had done all that lay in her power to deprive him of his birthright. He wrote an earnest letter to Elizabeth in the attempt to save his mother's life, but it was soon followed by a sort of apology and an intimation that all would be well if she would formally recognize him as her successor.

It is probable that there will always be two opinions in regard to the justice of Mary's execution.

"She fled to England for refuge," says one, "and should have been set free."

"To set her free would have been to deliver her up to the foes who would have taken her life," says the other, "or else to the friends who would have made war against England."

"A prisoner cannot be blamed for seeking liberty."

"But one may be justly punished for plotting treason."

"Mary was not a subject of the queen of England."

"He who commits treason is punished whether he is a subject or not."

"The testimony against her was false."

"It was sworn to by solemn oath. There was no other means of discovering the truth."

As to Elizabeth's real share in the execution of Mary there is quite as much difference of opinion.

"Because of her fear and jealousy she put to death the cousin to whom she had given every reason to expect protection," say the partisans of Mary.

"It shows little of either fear or jealousy to let her live for fifteen years," retort the supporters of Elizabeth.

"At least she signed the warrant with her own hand."

"Even a Tudor queen was not free to follow her own will. The English council had urged the deed for many years."

"Secretary Davison declared that she wished the warrant carried out."

"Davison told four different stories, and no one of them agreed with Elizabeth's version of the scene. Who shall tell where truth lies?"

"The warrant would have been worthless without her name."

"Walsingham's private secretary confessed many years afterwards that he forged the name at his master's command."

"Then why did she not deny the signature?"

"To whom? To James she did deny it as far as she dared. She wrote him that the execution was a 'miserable accident.' To her council she made no denial because the forger was the tool of the council, and had but carried out their will. Elizabeth could storm at her councilors, but, Tudor as she was, she had not the power to oppose their united determination." So the discussion has gone on for three hundred years.

The surest way for a wrongdoer to have his crimes forgotten and forgiven is to meet with dignity

Last moment of Mary, Queen of Scots.—*From painting by an unknown artist.*

and resignation the death that his deeds have made his lawful punishment. Whether Mary deserved this penalty or not, her calmness on the scaffold and her gentle submission to the death from which there was no escape have won friends and admirers for her even among the sternest critics of her life and her acts.

When the time was come for her execution, she went quietly to the hall of Fotheringay Castle, supported by two attendants, while a third bore her train. With a calm and cheerful face she stepped upon the low platform where lay the block. Platform, railing, block, and a low stool were heavily draped with black. She seated herself on the stool. On her right sat the two nobles to whom the charge of her execution had been committed, on her left stood the sheriff, and in front of her the two executioners, while around the railing stood many knights and other gentlemen who had come to see her die. Her robes belonged to the executioners, and when they began to remove her gown, as the custom was, she smiled and said she had never before been disrobed by such grooms. She had begged that some of her women might be with her to the last, and when they could no longer control themselves but began to weep and lament, she kissed them and said gently, "Do not weep, my friends, I have promised that you will not. Rejoice, for you will soon see an end of all your mistress's troubles." She repeated a Latin prayer, and then an English prayer for the church, for her son James, and for Queen Elizabeth, "that she might prosper and serve God aright." Her women pinned a linen cloth over her face. She knelt down upon the cushion and laid her head upon the block. "Into thy hands, O Lord, I commend my spirit," she cried, and so died Mary Stuart, Queen of Scotland and heir to the throne of England.

CHAPTER XV

THE SPANISH ARMADA

A N Englishman living in Lisbon hastened home to England and demanded audience with the queen.

"Your Majesty," said he, "King Philip is making great preparations for some warlike enterprise. In the Lisbon harbor are twenty galleons and forty other vessels. Men from Italy and Germany are coming in by hundreds. What can this mean but an attack upon England?"

Two months later came a message to the queen from her spies in Spain:—

"Soldiers are coming every day, and vast quantities of wine, grain, biscuit, bacon, oil, vinegar, barley meal, and salted meats are being laid in besides powder and cannon." A ship that had recently sailed from Lisbon was captured, and both captain and men were tortured on the rack that more might be learned of the doings of Philip. All told the same story, that he was planning an invasion of England.

In those days honor between sovereigns was a thing almost unknown. No one blamed the government of one country for trying to get the better of that of another. While Philip was making ready for war, he and Elizabeth were engaged in arranging for a treaty of peace and friendship. Each knew that the other was treacherous, but each meant to get the better of the bargain.

On the arrival of this news from Spain, Elizabeth sent for Drake. "Sir Francis," said she, "how would it please you to make a voyage to Spain?"

Drake guessed in a moment what she wished of him and answered most heartily:—

"There's nothing in all the world that would do me greater good."

"Ships and stores and soldiers are assembling off Cadiz and Lisbon. It would be a goodly sight, perhaps as fine as anything you saw in your voyage around the world."

"With how many ships may I go?" asked Drake.

"I can give you four, and the merchants will add to the fleet."

They did add twenty-six vessels of all kinds and sizes, for they well knew that, though Drake would probably sail with the usual orders to "do no harm to my good friend, the king of Spain," the chances were that every vessel would come back with a valuable cargo.

Drake made a rapid voyage, and on his return he at once brought his report to the queen.

"Well, my sailor lad," was her greeting, "have you another wild tale of adventure to tell me? Have you made me queen of a new land or have you excommunicated your chaplain?"

"I've not excommunicated my chaplain," returned Drake, "but it'll take many a blessing from the Pope to make up to the Spaniards for that merry time off Cadiz. I've not discovered a new country, but your Majesty is queen of what is stowed away in my ships, and perchance that is of more worth than some of the raw lands that lie to the westward."

Elizabeth's eyes shone. "I know you've been in many a gallant fight," said she, "and now tell me just what you have done."

"The Spanish fleet was off Cadiz ready to sail for Lisbon, so there was nothing else to do but to attack it. We took eighty or more of their vessels, laden with stores to the gunwale, and we captured two galleons."

"So that's the way you do no harm to my friend Philip," said the queen. "Brave sailor laddie that you are, what did you do next?"

"My men were a bit weary of the sea," answered Drake, "and——"

"Yes, it must have been a dull and wearisome voyage," said Elizabeth with a smile. "And what did you do to amuse them?"

"There was little to do, but we took three castles and burned some fishing boats and nets. I hadn't time for much, for there was news of a carrack coming from India, and it was only courtesy to sail out and give her a greeting."

"Surely," said the queen. "My sailors are always ready to show that kind of courtesy to an enemy in loneliness on the ocean."

"That's the whole story," said Drake, "save that the carrack was full of the richest treasure that ever sailed the seas, and I brought it home."

"That is more of your courtesy," said Elizabeth. "You would save the busy king from the care of it, I suppose."

"Yes, your Majesty. He'll be busy enough for one while. We've singed his whiskers for him."

The stories were true. Philip was at last determined to attack England. Mary was dead, and he claimed the crown by virtue of his connection with the royal house of Lancaster and by the will of the Queen of Scots. There was another side to his plan, Elizabeth had torn her country from its allegiance to the Pope, and this invasion was a crusade. If he conquered England, the country would be brought back to the Roman church, and so would Holland; it was a holy war. A Spanish cardinal wrote, "Spain does not war against Englishmen, but against Elizabeth. It is not England but her wretched queen who has overthrown the Holy Church and persecuted the pious Catholics. Let the English people rise and welcome their deliverer." This letter was circulated throughout England, but it produced no effect save to increase the loyalty of the English Catholics. They were the more indignant because the author of the letter was an Englishman who had abandoned his country and become a subject of Spain. "It is only the blast of a beggarly traitor," declared Elizabeth.

The "singeing of his whiskers" kept Philip waiting for a year. To sail out into the Atlantic with the probability of meeting the autumn gales far away from any friendly harbor would have been a reckless thing to do, and it was not easy to bring together at short notice stores enough to take the place of those that had been destroyed. Philip waited. He even gave the queen a final chance to avoid the attack, for he sent her a Latin verse to the effect that she might even yet escape his conquest by agreeing to return the treasure taken by Drake, to render no more aid to the Low Countries, and to bring her kingdom back to the Church of Rome. Elizabeth replied, "My good king, I'll obey you when the Greek kalends come around," and as the Greeks had no kalends, there was little hope of peace.

While the shipbuilders of Spain were working night and day, and while men and provisions and powder and cannon were being brought together, England, too, was preparing for the encounter. There was no ally on the continent to lend aid, the King of Scots might be faithful and he might not, according to what he regarded as for his interests. The fortifications of the kingdom were weak. At Portsmouth the guns could not be fired when the queen was crowned because the tower was so old and ready to crumble, and for thirty years little had been done to put it in order. This very weakness, however, of the resources of the government was England's strength, for every Englishman saw that if his country was to be saved from becoming a province of Spain, he and every other man must do his best to defend it. The council sent a message to London:—

"What number of ships and men is it your wish to contribute to the defence of the land?"

"How many may properly be required of us?" asked the Londoners.

"Fifteen ships and five thousand men," was the answer.

Now in all London there were hardly more than seventeen thousand men, but the city straightway wrote to the council:—

"Ten thousand men and thirty ships we will gladly provide, and the ships shall be amply furnished."

So it was throughout the kingdom. Every town sent a generous number of men and generous gifts of money. Every little village on the coast hastened to refit its fishing vessels and offer boats and sailors to the government. The wildest stories were rife of what the Spaniards would do if they were once in control of the country. It was said that they had already lists of the stately castles of the realm and the homes of rich London merchants, marked with the names of the Spanish nobles to whom they were to be given. Most of the English were to be hanged, so the rumor went, but all children under seven years of age were to be branded on the face and kept as slaves.

Philip had not expected to conquer England without other aid than that of the soldiers whom he was to carry with him. He had a large band of allies, on English soil, so he thought, waiting for his coming and ready to welcome him. These were the Catholics of England. The Pope had excommunicated Elizabeth and had pronounced the curse of the church upon all Catholics that should support her.

"These are not common days," said one of her advisers, "and in such times there must often be resort to means that would be most cruel and unjust in other years."

"What do you mean?" demanded the queen.

"Your Majesty has of course not failed to consider the support that the Spanish king may find if he succeeds in landing upon our shores."

"Who will support him, you or I?"

"It would be but natural for those of his own church to welcome him."

"They'll welcome him with powder and cannon."

"Your Majesty, when your illustrious father, King Henry VIII., was about to depart for the French wars, did he not bring to the block his own cousin and others who were most devoted to the old faith, lest they should raise an insurrection while he was on the continent?"

"And you would cut off the heads of my faithful subjects? They shall attend my church, and if they will not, they shall be fined or imprisoned. My agents are zealous, and it may be that they have sometimes gone beyond my orders, but I tell you that I rule men and women, not their thoughts, and if a man obeys me, his head stays on his shoulders, mark that. I'll tell you one thing more, the lord high-admiral of my fleet is to be Howard of Effingham. What think you of that, my man?"

"But, your Majesty, he is a strong supporter of the old faith."

"So will he be of the new queen," replied Elizabeth calmly.

Howard became admiral, and Drake vice-admiral, while Frobisher and Hawkins served as captains and Raleigh sailed out in his own vessel as a volunteer. Howard knew almost nothing of naval command, but around him were officers of experience, and he was not so exalted by his new dignity that he scorned to learn of them. The sailors watched him closely, and when they saw him put his own hands to the towing rope, they shouted "Hurrah for the admiral!" Nobles and commoners were mingled, and not one among them seemed to have any thought of rank or dignity. It was for England that they were working, and the honor lay in helping to save the country.

The English vessels came together. There were all sorts of craft, ranging from a ship not much smaller than the galleons of the Spaniards to what were hardly more than mere fishing boats. They were miserably supplied with food and powder, for it was very hard for Elizabeth to make up her mind to meet the vast expenses of war. Almost every letter of the admiral's contained a request for absolute necessities that were given out most grudgingly. Beef was too dear, thought the queen, and she changed the sailors' rations to a scanty supply of fish, oil, and peas. The wages were in arrears, there was not powder enough, food was carried to the ships in small quantities, though Howard declared indignantly, "King Harry never made a less supply than six weeks." At the least rumor that the Spaniards were not coming, Elizabeth would give orders to reduce the English fleet. The Invincible Armada had left Spain, and Howard wrote, "Beseech Burleigh to hasten provisions. If the wind holds out for six days, Spain will be knocking at our doors."

One evening in July a game of bowls was going on at the Pelican Inn in Plymouth.

"Your turn, Frobisher," said Hawkins, "and then Sir Walter's."

"That's well done, Sir Walter. Yours next, Sir Francis," said Howard. Drake stooped for the ball, and was about to send it, when an old sailor rushed into the room and cried:—

"Admiral, Admiral, they're coming! I saw them off the Lizard, and there are hundreds of them."

"What do you say, Admiral," asked Drake with his hand still on the ball, "Won't there be time to finish the game and then go out and give the dons a thrashing?"

The Spanish ships slowly made their way into the Channel. They were so large and so high at stem and stern that they looked like great floating-castles, but they were so clumsy and difficult to manage that the nimble little English boats had a great advantage.

The Spanish Armada attacked by the English Fleet. *From Pine's engraving of the tapestry, formerly in the House of Lords, but destroyed by fire in the eighteenth century.*

The Spanish fleet formed in a wide crescent, the two points seven miles apart, and the English boats went out to meet them. The galleons were high and the English vessels so low that it was difficult to train the Spanish guns upon them, moreover, the Spaniards were not good marksmen. They would have had a better chance, however, if the English had only been willing to stand still and be fired at, but the Spanish were much surprised and disgusted when the saucy little English craft slipped up under their very bows, fired a shot or two and were away firing at the next ship before the Spanish guns could be trained upon them. Some of the little boats sailed the whole length of the crescent, firing at every vessel and coming off without a scar.

This kind of encounter was kept up for more than a week, for the English hesitated to attempt a regular engagement. The Spanish suffered severely. Masts were shattered, the rigging was cut up, great, ragged holes were torn in the hulls, and large numbers of sailors were slain, but even worse was to follow.

The Spaniards were anchored off Calais. At two o'clock one morning a strange, shapeless object was seen floating toward them. Then came another and another until there were eight. Fire blazed up from the floating monsters. There were explosions and suffocating gases. The flames rose higher, wind and waves were bringing these malignant creatures, that seemed half alive, into the midst of the Spanish fleet.

This attack by fire-boats was a new way of fighting. The Spaniards were perplexed and horrified. Their only thought was to escape anywhere, no matter where, if only they could get free from these terrors. In their haste anchor chains fouled, some ships collided, others burned or ran aground.

The land forces were encamped at Tilbury. "I am commander in chief of my troops," declared Elizabeth, "and I shall go to pay them a visit."

"Is it safe to commit yourself to armed multitudes? Among so many there may well be treachery," suggested her councilors.

"Let tyrants fear," returned Elizabeth. "I am true to my people, and they are my faithful and loving subjects. I should rather die than live in fear and distrust of them. I shall go to visit my loyal soldiers."

It must have been a brilliant sight, the long lines of soldiers in battle array, and the queen riding in front of the lines on her great charger. Before her went Leicester and another noble bearing the sword of state. Behind her followed a page carrying her helmet with its white plumes. She was magnificently dressed, but over her dress was a corslet of polished steel. Back and forth before the lines she rode, while the soldiers shouted, "Queen Elizabeth! Queen Elizabeth! God save the queen! The Lord keep her!" She raised her hand, and there was silence to hear her words.

"I have the body of a weak, feeble woman," she said, "but I have the heart of a king, of a king of England, and I think it foul scorn that any prince of Europe should dare to invade the borders of my realm. Rather than that any dishonor should come by me, I will take up arms, I will be your general myself, and the rewarder of every deed of bravery. You deserve already rewards and crowns, and they shall be paid. It will not be long before we have a famous victory over these enemies of my God, of my kingdom, and of my people."

While Elizabeth was still at Tilbury, two messengers came with a thrilling report.

"A fierce battle has been fought off Gravelines. Drake was in command."

"My noble sailor laddie," said the queen proudly. "Tell me of it. I would know the deeds of every one of my brave captains."

"It is your Majesty who struck the fatal blow," said the messenger, "for the fire-ships were your own thought, and it was they that thrust the Spaniards from our coast and drove them out to sea. Sir Francis and his fleet led the attack. Six hours it lasted, till every shot, large and small, had been fired. Then came the Admiral, and he, too, fired every shot. There was no more powder, but he put on a bold front and gave them chase. They could not go south, and they went north."

"There's no fear in Howard," said Elizabeth. "I know my man. Where are the Spaniards now?"

"Many of them have gone to whatever place the mercy of the Lord may consign them," was the reply.

"And where are those that still depend upon the mercies of wind and wave?" asked the queen.

"Only wind and wave can tell!" answered the messenger. "The ships sailed far to the northward. The Admiral pursued until his provisions failed, but there was small need of searching for the enemy. The boisterous northern seas will do the work of many a cannon."

The words of the messenger proved to be true. The Spanish ships ran aground on the unknown coasts, they were shattered by storms, the sailors were stricken by pestilence, they were driven ashore only to be thrust back into the waves, for King James had no idea of doing aught against the sovereign whose crown he hoped would before many years rest upon his own head, and the lord lieutenant of Ireland was little inclined to show mercy to the enemies of his country. Of the great fleet that left Spain, so strong that it ventured to call itself invincible, more than half the ships were left on the rocks or at the bottom of the sea.

CHAPTER XVI

CLOSING YEARS

A FTER the defeat of the Armada not only was there a general rejoicing, but the whole land felt a new sense of freedom. Until 1588 Elizabeth had been obliged to steer the ship of state with the utmost wariness. She must keep on good terms with Scotland, lest that country should turn to France for friendship. She must make sure that France would not oppose her, lest Philip should join the ruler of the land across the Channel. She must help the Low Countries sufficiently to strengthen their opposition to the Spanish king and so keep him from England, but she must not give them so much aid that they would become a burden upon her in their dependence, and she must not accept the Protectorate, that would perhaps involve her realm in a long and bloody war with Spain. For thirty years this keen, shrewd scheming went on. England was gaining every day in power and wealth, and when at last "Old Leadenfoot" began to bestir himself, the country was ready to meet him.

The Armada had come and gone, and England was free. Philip might talk as boastfully as he would about sending another fleet to make another attack, but no one forgot that he had sent a fleet and it had failed. England was "mistress of the seas" in the sense that she was no longer in fear of any other nation. If a Spanish vessel encountered an English vessel, they would be likely to fight, but the Englishmen expected to win, and that expectation of victory was in itself a mark of greatness. If England chose to plant colonies in the New World, there was little fear that Spain would trouble them to any great extent.

This new sense of freedom showed itself not only in what was done but in what was written, and often the same man that had written an undying poem could fight a battle or lead a voyage of discovery or plan what was best for the nation when there were difficult questions of state to decide. Shakespeare himself, the greatest writer of all, was not only a poet but a keen, thrifty man of business.

The people of England had become accustomed to seeing great deeds done before their eyes, and that is one reason why few stories were written but many plays, for it seemed much more "real" to see a tale acted on the stage than to hear an account of it.

It was a great pity that this freedom could not have extended to religious matters, but it was some years after Queen Elizabeth's death before many people realized that it was possible for two persons to have entirely different ideas of religion and yet be honest and sincere and live peacefully together. Toward the close of Elizabeth's reign there were persecutions of those refusing to attend the Church of England that were far more severe than the mild system of fines with which she began her rule. The fines were increased, and Puritans as well as Catholics were sometimes ruined by the large sums of money that they were obliged to pay if they persisted in refusing to attend the services of the Church of England. They were often imprisoned, and in the Elizabethan days imprisonment was no light penalty. Not only were the jails damp, unhealthy, filthy places, but prisoners were obliged to pay many exorbitant charges, so that if a man escaped with his life and health, he had to leave large sums of money behind him. One jail bill of that day has a weekly item of five dollars and a half for food, and as money would purchase about five times as much then as now, this charge was equivalent to more than twenty-seven dollars to-day. This was not all by any means, for a prisoner had to pay the rent of his wretched dungeon. If he was doomed to wear fetters, he must pay extra for them, and, most absurd charge of all, he was forced to pay an entrance fee on being sent to the horrible place. Besides being imprisoned, dissenters, as those were called who would not attend the Church of England, were sometimes whipped or tortured or even hanged. The only excuse for such treatment is that neither the queen nor her council was in fault for not being a century in advance of their times. Indeed, it was more than two centuries after the death of the queen before England would allow a Catholic to become a member of Parliament.

As Elizabeth drew older, she dressed with increasing magnificence. Her hands were loaded with rings, and her robes were made of the richest material that could be obtained. A German traveler who saw her on her way to her private chapel describes her as wearing a dress of heavy white silk, made with a very long train and bordered with pearls as large as beans. She wore a deep collar made of gold and jewels. This same traveler says that every corner of her palace shone with gold and silver and crystal and precious stones, and yet her floors were strewn with rushes that were probably as dirty as those in the homes of her subjects.

The end of the century drew near, and it brought sorrow to the queen in the death of her old adviser, Lord Burleigh. Leicester had died soon after the defeat of the Armada, and Elizabeth never parted with a paper upon which she had written sadly, "His last letter." In Burleigh's old age he became quite infirm, and while Elizabeth's other ministers addressed her kneeling, Burleigh was always made to seat himself comfortably before she would discuss any question with him. "I am too old and too feeble to serve you well," he would say, but she refused to let him resign his office. In the days of his strength, she would storm at him in a tornado of rage when his judgment differed from hers, but as he became weak and ill, she was the tenderest of friends. "The door is low, your Majesty," said the servant as she entered the sickroom of the councilor. "Then I will stoop," said she, "for your master's sake, though never for the king of Spain." She often went to sit by his bedside, and the haughty sovereign whose wrath burst forth so furiously at a word of opposition became the most gentle of nurses. As she sat beside him, she would allow no hand but her own to give him nourishment. "She never speaks of him without tears," said one who was with her after his death.

The loss of another of her friends brought her even greater grief than that of Burleigh, for this time the life of her favorite lay in her own power, but as the faithful sovereign she felt herself obliged to sacrifice it. From the time that Leicester had presented to her his brilliant, fascinating stepson, the Earl of Essex, the young man had been a prime favorite with the queen. At their first meeting he was seventeen and the queen fifty-six, and she treated him like a petted child who can do no wrong. She forbade him to take any part in the fighting in Portugal, but he slipped away from court without her knowledge, and was the first to leave the boats on the Portuguese coast. He returned with some fear of being punished for his disobedience, but the queen forgot the wrongdoing, and was only anxious to make up for his disappointment because a position that he had wished for had been given to some one else.

When Essex married, Elizabeth was as indignant as usual at each new proof that with all the adoration that her courtiers continually declared of herself, she was not the whole world to them. When Essex was fighting in Holland, a request was sent to the queen for more troops. The ambassador said:—

"Your Majesty, my master has consulted the Earl of Essex, and he favors the request."

Elizabeth had not yet granted Essex her forgiveness, and she blazed forth:—

"The Earl of Essex, indeed! He would have it thought that he rules my realm."

In spite of her anger with him, she was so anxious when she knew how carelessly he risked his life that she wrote ordering him to return to England at once, and when, much against his will, he obeyed her command, she spent a week in feasting and merriment. Over and over they quarreled. Essex would perhaps favor one candidate for a position, and the queen another. There would be hot words between them, and they would part, both in a fury. Then Essex would pretend to be ill, and the repentant queen would go to see the spoiled child, and pardon his petulance unasked. "He is not to blame, he takes it from his mother," she would say, and as she especially disliked his mother, she admitted this as sufficient excuse for overlooking his impertinence. The great storm came when the queen named a lord lieutenant for Ireland, and Essex opposed. Elizabeth made one of her severe speeches, and the young man retorted by shrugging his shoulders and turning his back on her. The queen replied by soundly boxing his ears. Essex grasped his sword. "I wouldn't have pardoned that blow even from King Henry himself. What else could one expect from an old king in petticoats!" he cried and dashed away from court.

His friends urged him to return and try to regain the affection of the queen by a humble apology, but for many weeks he refused. "I am the queen's servant," said he, "but I am not her slave." However, he finally sued for pardon and was again forgiven.

So long as the offences of Essex were against Elizabeth as a woman, she was ready to forgive, but at last he committed a crime against her government, and the woman was forgotten in the sovereign. All through the reign there was trouble with Ireland. The Irish hated the English and would follow anyone who would lead them against English rule. There were continual rebellions. Essex's enemies brought it about that the favorite should be sent to command what he called "the cursedest of all islands." Before long, rumors of his mismanagement began to reach the ears of the queen. "He is ever forcing his soldiers to make wearisome and useless marches and countermarches," said the reports. "He wastes money and supplies, and he exhausts his troops by irregular skirmishes that amount to nothing. He has made a foolish peace with the leader of the Irish rebels instead of suppressing them by force of arms. He is trying to make himself king of the Irish, and he will then raise an Irish army to come over and dethrone the queen."

Elizabeth sent letters full of reproof to Essex, but the young fellow only said to himself, "They are not her letters. She has written the words, but it is Burleigh who has guided her pen." He abandoned his command and went straight to England, sure that the queen would pardon any misdeed on the part of her favorite.

Early one morning the young man arrived in London. He must see the queen before his enemies could have word of her and induce her to forbid him to appear at court, and he galloped wildly on to the palace. He looked into the audience chamber, she was

221

not there; into the privy chamber, she was not there. Then he burst into her dressing room where the queen sat with her women brushing her hair. He was muddy with his mad gallop to the palace, his clothes were disordered and travelstained, but when he threw himself at her feet and pleaded, "Don't judge me by the tales of my enemies," the queen was so kind to him that he thought himself forgiven. Later, however, she saw that he had committed many acts of disobedience which in a military commander were unpardonable. He was tried by the privy council, and for a few weeks was confined to his own house. Elizabeth deprived him of several valuable monopolies and even after his release forbade him to appear at court. In any other commander the penalty of such crimes would have been far more severe, but instead of thinking upon the mercy that had been shown him, Essex meditated upon what he thought his wrongs. He became more and more embittered, and at last he tried to arouse a rebellion against the queen. There was a fierce struggle in Elizabeth's mind between her love for the young man and her duty to punish the treason. At last she signed the death warrant, recalled it, then signed another, and Essex was executed in the Tower of London.

The seventeenth century began, and the health of the queen was clearly failing. A woman of less strength of character would have posed as an invalid, but Elizabeth seemed to feel that sickness was unworthy of a queen, and she concealed her increasing weakness as far as possible. She often had to be lifted upon her horse, but she would not give up riding. She even went to visit one of her councilors. Cornets saluted her, drums and trumpets sounded as she entered the courtyard. She watched the dancing of the ladies of the house and the feats of horsemanship and swordplay of the young men, but she was exhausted, and in spite of her good courage, she could not go up the stairs without a staff. Yet in the early part of 1602 she went a-Maying in the old fashion of celebrating the coming of spring.

With all her glory and her greatness, the last days of this woman on a throne were more lonely than those of a woman in a cottage. Essex had been a great favorite among the people, and they had never forgiven his death. When the queen showed herself among them, she was no longer received with all the old tokens of loyalty and affection, and no one could have been more keen than she to note the least change in the manner of her subjects.

She knew that James would be her heir, but she had not forgotten the long lines of greedy courtiers who had sought her when her sister Mary was near her end, and she refused to name him definitely as the one whom she wished to succeed her. This refusal made little difference, however, in the increasing devotion of those around her to the Scotch king, who would so soon be the ruler of England. One after another wearied of attendance; some made excuses to leave her, others left without excuse. The son of Burleigh, who had taken his father's place, sent almost daily epistles to Scotland. Harington, who used to write her merry, jesting letters, signed "Your Majesty's saucy godson," had sent valuable gifts to the King of Scots, and a petition that he might not be forgotten when James should come into his kingdom. Her own councilors were sending messengers to James hoping to win his favor. Two of her relatives stood by her bedside, but their watchfulness arose not from affection but that they might be the first to tell James that the crown was his at last.

The queen became more and more feeble. She was sad and melancholy. Often she sat for hours alone in the dark weeping. She felt her loneliness most keenly. "Whom can I trust? Whom can I trust?" her attendants heard her murmur. A kinsman who went to see her said that she drew heavy sighs continually, "And I never knew her to sigh," he declared, "save at the death of the Queen of Scots." She lay on cushions piled up on the floor.

"Madam," urged the son of Burleigh, "will you not be moved to your bed?"

"If I go to my bed, I shall never leave it," she answered.

"But you must in order to content your loving subjects," he urged.

Then the queen showed once more her proud Tudor blood. " 'Must' is no word to use to princes," said she, "and, little man, if your father had lived, even he would not have dared to say so much."

She passed away quietly in a gentle sleep. According to a strange custom of the times an image of her was made in wax, decked in the royal robes, and laid upon her coffin. She was buried in Westminster

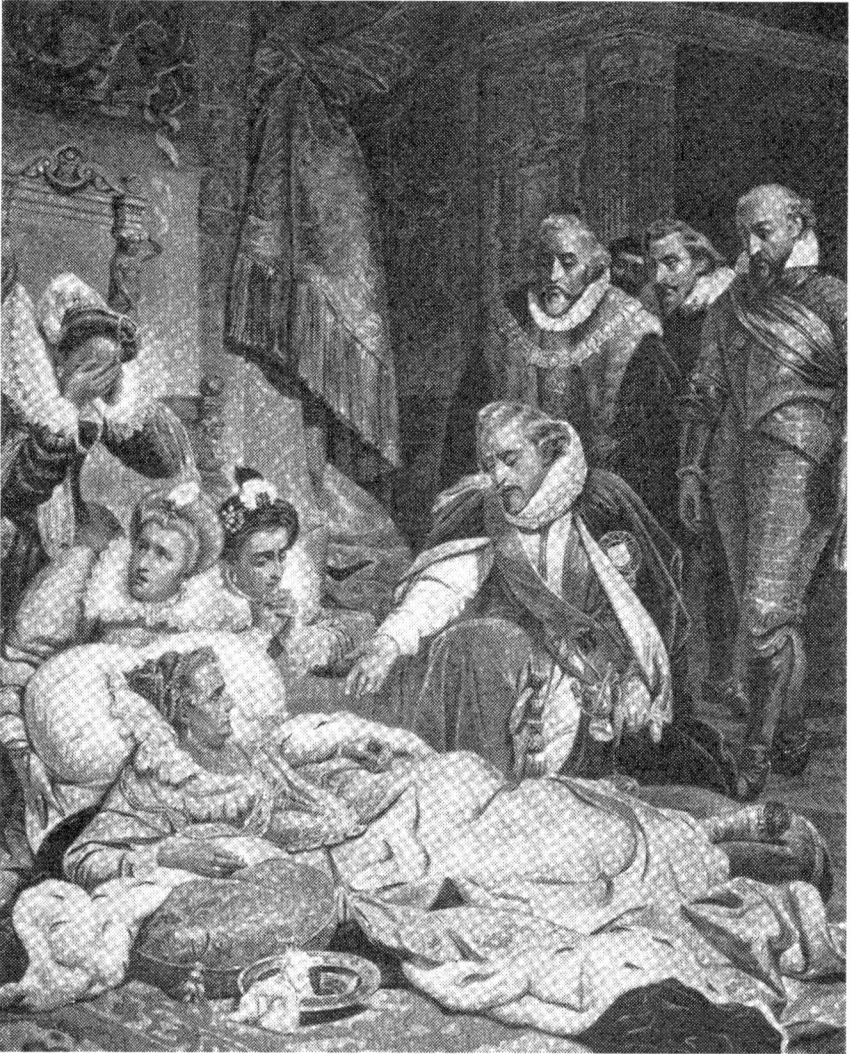

Last moments of Elizabeth.—*From painting by Delaroche.*

Abbey, and as the sad procession went through the streets, the early love of her subjects returned in full measure. An old chronicler says:—

"And when they beheld her statue, or effigy, lying on the coffin, set forth in royal robes, having a crown upon the head thereof, and a ball and sceptre in either hand, there was such a general sighing, groaning, and weeping, as the like hath not been seen or known in the memory of man; neither doth any history mention any people, time, or state, to make like lamentation for the death of their sovereign."

www.ingramcontent.com/pod-product-compliance
Lightning Source LLC
Chambersburg PA
CBHW031832090426
42741CB00005B/221